OUT OF THE PIT!

Overcoming the Self-Sabotage

of Depression and Anxiety

Susan F. Tackett, LCPC

Susan F. Tackett

I have endeavored to share my story as I perceive it actually happened, which means that various portrayals are admittedly subjective and not always flattering. Because my intention is not to malign anyone, I have either omitted or changed the names of certain individuals, locations, and institutions.

Unless otherwise noted, all scripture quotes are taken from the *New International Version of the Holy Bible*, Zondervan Bible Publishers, Copyright © 1978. Other quotations are from the *New American Standard Bible*, Copyright © 1973 The Lockman Foundation, and from *The Holy Bible, King James Version*, Copyright © 1966 by Royal Publishers, Inc.

ISBN 0-9674266-0-X

Excerpts from the GROW blue book are used by permission of Con Keogh and GROW International.

Excerpts from *Front Porch Tales* are used by permission of Multnomah Publishers, Inc.

All highlighting within quotes and excerpts is mine.

Cover design by Nellie Fleiss.

I waited patiently for the Lord;

he turned to me and heard my cry.

He lifted me out of the slimy pit,

out of the mud and mire;

He set my feet on a rock

and gave me a firm place to stand.

He put a new song in my mouth,

a hymn of praise to our God.

Psalm 40:1-3

I am a survivor - and more than that - an overcomer. Fifteen years ago, I survived a major depression that included a five-week stay in a psychiatric unit. This experience forever changed and enriched my life. Since then I have become a Licensed Clinical Professional Counselor and have had the privilege of helping others to recover. In this account I share my experience with still other fellow sufferers, so that they too may survive, overcome, and sing a new song.

Contents

But we have this treasure in jars of clay
to show that this all-surpassing power is
from God and not from us.
We are hard pressed on every side, but not crushed;
perplexed, but not in despair;
persecuted, but not abandoned;
struck down, but not destroyed.
We know that the one who raised the Lord Jesus
from the dead will also raise us with Jesus
and present us with you in his presence.
Therefore we do not lose heart.
For our light and momentary troubles
are achieving for us an eternal glory
that far outweighs them all.

2 Cor. 4:7-9, 14, 16-17

5

Acknowledgements

My first words of thanks go to my husband, Ray, for his prayer support, his encouragement, and the many meals he prepared while I was dividing my time between book-writing and counseling; and most of all, for accepting me and loving me for who I am. Thanks also go to all my sons, who have been telling me for years that I should write my story. And I owe an enormous debt of gratitude to Daddy, Mama, Joe, David, and Vanessa, each of whom in their own way contributed so much to the typing or printing of this manuscript that I couldn't have produced the final product without them. Thank you, Sarah, for your enthusiasm, your prayers, and your ideas (included in Chapter 23).

Many others have also played a part in getting this material into print, so I want to acknowledge you here: Luci Swindoll, without whose "Take a Risk" message the project might never have gotten off the ground; Gary and Mona, without whom I never would have heard Luci; Traci Mullins, who helped me begin to put my ideas on paper; Rosemary, Connie, David, Michelle, Cathy, Denise, Judy, Cyndi, Pat, Kay, and the rest of you who have prayed faithfully for me and for this book, and each of my clients who provided me the invaluable service of critiquing the manuscript; Bettye, for help in securing publishing information; Nellie, for designing the book cover; the CCFS staff and board for supporting me in this endeavor and accommodating my crazy schedule; and—from my healing time—GROW, Inc., for providing me with people and a program to help me do just that; Denise B, my friend and mentor; and our church family, who patiently supported all of us while I was "in the pit."

And to God: I promised you that if you would heal and sustain me, I would give you the credit and the glory; this I do with a thankful heart!

Susan Tackett, August 1999

PART ONE:

INTRODUCTION

To give you hope and a future....

Jeremiah 29:11

To my hurting friend:

If you feel hopeless, confused, and desperate, this letter is to you. My heart goes out to you.

Your particular kind of suffering may feel too vague and baffling to have a name. However, if your experience is like mine, it does have a name, or maybe two. **For me, they were "clinical depression" and "anxiety," and they threatened to swallow me up.**

Have you noticed that when someone asks how you are, you are almost not up to answering, in spite of your need to be understood? Words seem pitifully inadequate. Even if you do bend the person's ear for a while, do you still feel that you haven't fully conveyed your actual state?

There's a scene in the movie "Forrest Gump" in which Forrest and Jenny, adults now, are standing in front of her dilapidated childhood home. As she remembers the abuse she experienced there, she begins to hurl rocks at the house. Then she collapses on the ground, crying tears of rage and grief. Forrest comments, "Sometimes I guess there just aren't enough rocks."

When it comes to severe depression and anxiety, sometimes there just aren't enough WORDS. Or the right words. No description does justice to such anguish.

Allow me to try to put your experience into words by sharing a little of my own remembered pain. Perhaps as you see the similarity in our experiences, you will at least feel understood and not so alone. Perhaps some of your fear that you are weird or incurable will be dispelled. And maybe, just maybe, you will see a pinpoint of light at the top of the pit, as you realize that somebody who was as miserable as you are truly did recover.

In 1984 I was hospitalized for the treatment of major depression and panic disorder. I was sick and frightened and barely functioning as a wife and mother. My emotions owned me.

How do you feel right now? Despondent? Bewildered? Scarcely able to remember what it was like to feel good? Haunted by the fear that you will only get worse?

If you are clinically depressed, your eating and sleeping routines may be out of whack. Nothing brings you much pleasure. Do you find that you honestly don't care very much about things you once considered important? Do you catch yourself thinking, "I am just not myself"? If you are irritable, or if you have needed a lot of reassurance and help around the house, you suspect that your family is getting tired of you; you may have even entertained thoughts of relieving them of the burden.

If you are plagued by anxiety, you may be restless or fidgety or have episodes of intense panic. You may worry and obsess without any ability to stop the thoughts. In fact, your internal brakes are worn thin - you may cry rivers of tears, or fly into rages, or talk in circles.

You wonder if even God understands how profoundly miserable you are. If so, why doesn't He do something about it? You pray, but you don't feel much better. It hurts when someone questions your faith, though at times you wonder if they have a point. In my case, I was a pastor's wife, aware that I was being observed by many people who were concerned and disappointed that I wasn't getting myself together.

Do you feel a bizarre eeriness sometimes - as if things around you are not real, or perhaps you are not real? Does it seem like a cloud settles over your mind and spirit? Do you feel mentally foggy or detached from reality? Possibly you feel rather disconnected from everybody, even God. You may have isolated yourself from other people, or at least withdrawn inside yourself when they are around. You may feel remote even from yourself – you look in the mirror and simply don't connect with the image.

You probably have been trying for some time to figure out what's wrong, and you have tried all the solutions you can think of. You wonder if anyone else has ever felt this peculiar kind of torment, or if you are unique. If the advice you receive from other people doesn't seem relevant, you may feel alarmed that nobody seems to have any real answers. If you have physical symptoms, and no medical cause has been found, you are even more concerned. Does this mean the doctors don't know what to do either?

You're tired of being victimized by something you can't put your finger on. Your own thoughts and attitudes do seem to have something to do with it, but are they the cause or the result? There are no molehills, only mountains. Everything takes so much effort. Getting out of bed hardly seems worth it, yet staying in bed doesn't ensure that you will feel rested.

You feel stuck; you are pedalling frantically but going nowhere and becoming more discouraged and weary. Does anyone appreciate how hard you are trying to overcome this?

I experienced almost all of these things, and for such a long time that I added doubting and anger to the load. I remember it all very well, because the emotions were so strong, and because everything about the experience seemed so significant to me.

God was listening after all. The Comforter and Counselor was with me even when I didn't feel His presence, and He is with you, too.

I did recover fully, though gradually. I went to graduate school and have been counseling professionally since 1992. The truth of Romans 8:28 has been demonstrated in my life: God turned one of my worst times into one of the best, both for me personally and for the lives I have since been able to touch.

II Corinthians 1:3-4 expresses my conviction well: our God is "the Father of compassion and the God of all comfort, who comforts us in all our troubles, **so that we can comfort those in any trouble with the comfort we ourselves have received from God."** **God didn't heal me just for my own sake or my family's, but for yours.** Who knows what He will do with you in the lives of others? Actually, God knows; He can see that far even if you can't.

God's promises apply not just to me, but to you. Start with this one in Jeremiah 29:11-14: "For I know the plans I have for you," declares the Lord, "plans to prosper you and not to harm you, plans to give you hope and a future. Then you will call upon me and come and pray to me, and I will listen to you. You will seek me and find me when you seek me with all your heart. **I will be found by you," declares the Lord, "and will bring you back from captivity."** **God can deliver you from this bondage. Take this to heart.**

Your depression or anxiety state may be different from what I experienced, with different symptoms, or more or fewer of them. If your condition is not as critical as mine was, be grateful, but **the same stumbling blocks may hinder you and the same lessons apply**.

If you are in as dire straits as I was, you may not feel any better after reading this little bit, but do bear with me. **If you need to borrow confidence and vision from someone else for a while, then hang on to mine.**

With great hope for you,
Susan Tackett

P. S. If you are in the deepest part of the "pit" right now, you should probably read the book straight through. If you have already begun climbing out of the pit and you fear that reading about my worst days could threaten a setback for you, I suggest that you read the first two chapters, skim the highlighted parts only in chapters 3 through 6, and resume reading with chapter 7; you can always return to 3 through 6 later.

"Peace, peace, to those far and near,"
says the Lord.
"And I will heal them."
Isaiah 57:19b

PART TWO:

THE PIT

Turning stumbling blocks into stepping stones

No pit is so deep

that God's love is not

deeper still.

Corrie ten Boom

I do not believe that you have consciously caused your own depression or anxiety. Even if you gain attention of some kind while you are feeling down, I imagine you want to be healthy and whole more than you want to cling to anything you gain by being sick.

However, if you are like I was, you inadvertently allow things to keep you stuck, so that you may have become *your own worst enemy* without even realizing it.

The list of potential stumbling blocks is long:

> **lethargy or inertia,
> **physical illness,
> **denial or defensiveness,
> **misguided stubbornness or pride,
> **situations which sidetrack you,
> **people who seem to deliberately
>   undermine you,
> **resentment or self-pity,
> **skepticism or distrust,
> **lack of information or self-awareness,
> **faulty beliefs and assumptions,
> **a distorted view of reality,
> **twisted thought patterns,
> **doubts and unanswered questions,
> **overwhelming emotions,
> **impatience, and, last but not least,
> **your own sense that nothing is going
>   to make any difference anyway.

Any of these can hinder your recovery and even set you back.

I have observed that many of the "but's," "what if's," and "if only's" that obstructed my way out of the pit have posed a problem for my clients as well. They may sabotage you, too.

So imagine that you and I are sitting together and swapping experiences. **The bulk of what I have to share comes from the five weeks and two days of my 1984 psychiatric hospitalization**. These were intense weeks. It seems incredible even to me that I learned and changed so much during this time until I remember that I experienced about a year's worth of therapy concentrated into this much shorter period. This was a pivotal time in my life, so much so that I measure every event in my life by whether it happened "before St. Mark's" or "after St. Mark's."

As I tell my story and you climb with me out of the darkness, I will be sharing with you some steps for overcoming the obstacles, because - and this is the good news - you have some degree of control over most of them. And **every time you surmount a stumbling block, it becomes a step which puts you a little nearer to the light**. I hope you find something you can use to get out of your own pit.

Chapter 1

Where Did This Begin?

Before we focus on climbing out of the pit, let's take a brief look at my background. This may help you in two ways: **noting the precursors of depression and anxiety in my life may help you spot the precursors in your own, and seeing the strengths or positives in my life may help you identify your own.** Many adult sufferers of depression or anxiety share common background factors, for example, the same basic temperament or similar early experiences. Positives or plusses are also worth noting, because they are relevant to over-all adjustment and recovery. **As you ponder how you are going to recover, do not overlook any resources which you already have available.**

Here's what I found in looking back:

My baby pictures show a smiling, chubby-cheeked infant who was the very picture of health. No sign of neurosis there.

My childhood was happy and trauma-free. Both of my parents were loving, and I was close to each of them. They encouraged me in every area of my life, never holding me back due to my gender, and they provided a foundation of appropriate discipline. Many sufferers like myself experienced a relatively normal, happy childhood, but many did not.

My mother seemed very strong to me; I would have challenged anyone who questioned my mother's ability to solve any and every problem. My dad had his own struggles with depression and anxiety, but my only awareness was that from time to time he was feeling "sick." I did not feel any less secure during these times, which seemed brief to me.

My mother had early concerns that I was too shy. When I was a preschooler we had no close neighbors, so she invited other children over from time to time to make sure I was properly socialized. I wasn't terribly thrilled about having company. I was content being with family, which included a younger sister, Sarah, by my third birthday.

My mother registered me for school at the expected time, even though I was small physically and would be the youngest in my class. I think she had reservations about this but hoped the social setting would be good for me. I remember taking school very seriously from the outset, setting my sights on straight A's and never wavering.

I don't remember much about my classmates in the first grade, but I remember a great deal after that, mostly because I made a good friend in the second grade who drew me out of my shell. Rosemary was the kind of friend that whole books are written about. We are still good friends.

My family attended church and Sunday School weekly. My mother said bedtime prayers with me, and as I grew up, spontaneous praying came naturally to me, though I must admit I was most inclined to pray when I was in a crisis. I came to know Christ as a child; I cannot say exactly how old I was, but I know that God was largely an abstraction at the time, and it was Jesus who was real to me. I did consciously try to live as the Bible said I should. I had a sensitive conscience and really winced when I knew I had sinned. For that matter, I felt a deep sense of shame any time I let someone down or failed at something. We had high standards in my home, but I seem to have raised these another notch or two myself, as in my obsession with straight A's.

One of my mother's goals was for me to be "well-rounded," so she saw to it that I participated in a variety of activities, learned new skills, and developed my talents, especially playing the piano.

17

My dad was equally loving and put the icing on the cake, so to speak. He fostered in me a love of words, names, and paper-and-pencil games. He helped me with science and social studies projects, encouraged me in the safe use of my chemistry set, and pointed out the constellations in the night sky. I have fond memories of my dad standing with me in the yard, looking up at the stars, just as I recall the warmth of sitting beside my mother as she read stories to me when I was younger.

Throughout grade school I continued to be shy around strangers and lacking in self-confidence around my peers, except in the areas of music and academics where I did feel adequate. My feelings were easily hurt, and I avoided situations where I might feel humiliated. I feared rowdy outdoor group activities because of my frailty, and I dreaded settings such as Girl Scouts where my lack of certain skills would be evident. I preferred playing word games, working puzzles, reading, writing poetry, or exploring the out-of-doors with an eye for "scientific discoveries." I enjoyed our pets and our piano, where I could really let go and express myself. I also enjoyed my baby brother David, who was my buddy. I was as proud as if he were my own.

I cannot remember life without a nervous stomach or the fear of the dark. I was impressionable and easily frightened, and the hearing of my first ghost story around age seven dramatically affected my life. At night I lay in bed terrified, finding no comfort whatsoever in knowing that a severed hand could not actually be scratching on my window screen.

The teen years.

My difficulty falling asleep lasted through my high school years. Even when I had ceased to dwell on the ghost story, my imagination kept me awake for hours, either worrying about something or composing poetry. My mental brakes didn't seem to work. My junior high years were the worst in this regard.

Junior high was rough in other ways, too. I felt self-conscious and inadequate. These feelings were made worse by the fact that I still looked like a little girl. I thought puberty would never arrive. I was as uncomfortable in Home Ec as in P.E., though for different reasons. I'd had plenty of opportunities to learn things like cooking and sewing, but I was disinterested in these activities, and it showed.

In spite of all this I was basically happy, had many other interests, and felt good about my accomplishments. I did have friends and was voted "Most Courteous" in my grade.

I was excited when my family moved to Illinois the summer before my sophomore year. This move turned out to be good for me, in that I resolved not to be deterred from my goal to be valedictorian, and thereby had to overcome some of my timidity. Such a pursuit required boldness in this much-larger school, as well as a willingness to be teased. My new peers were already somewhat amused by this Arkansas hillbilly, so I was determined to humbly put them in their place. A steady boyfriend, John, and the camaraderie of our high school band also boosted my self-confidence.

I continued to have a nervous stomach, which could more accurately be called a "serious" or "intense" stomach. When I was preoccupied and in earnest pursuit of something, I had difficulty eating, whether or not I actually felt nervous. As a result, for most of high school I didn't eat much breakfast or lunch.

I do not remember feeling anything like depression during my childhood or adolescence. The most intense emotion I felt was anger, which escalated to rage when I felt torn between my protective mother and unsympathetic John. I do not know if my rage was pathological or just a natural extreme of adolescence; it was definitely a contrast to the peaceable nature I had exhibited prior to that time. I do know that I was developing my own identity as a separate person, distinct from my mother, a process which occasionally resulted in strain and conflict between us.

From college to motherhood.

After graduating as class valedictorian, I went to college back in Arkansas, where I had many friends and two primary interests - keeping up my grades and maintaining a long-distance relationship with John. I studied so late at night in my pursuit of academic excellence that I finally had no trouble dropping off to sleep. During a break-up with John, I enjoyed dating around; then he and I made up.

When I married John at age 20, I had no reservations that he was the man for me, though I did hope he would outgrow certain tendencies. I'm sure he hoped I would improve in some areas, too. I had never cooked an entire meal in my life (due to my lack of interest), and he put up with a lot while I was learning.

During our first two years of marriage we experienced stress due to my parents splitting up. Besides that, the only personal problem I had was with what I can best call separation anxiety, similar to the longing I felt as a child when I went away to camp, only more intense. It overtook me on three or four occasions when John left the house to attend a meeting at the church, which was just next door. One or two of these times we were in the middle of an unresolved argument, but that does not sufficiently explain the urgency I felt as I clung to him, nor does our having been apart for three years of college prior to marriage. We were both puzzled.

I liked being married, and John and I had wonderful times together. Our lives were eventful: college graduation for me, substitute teaching, the excitement of a pregnancy, and John's college graduation. We moved to Denver so that he could attend

20

seminary. I was enthralled by the Rockies and utterly delighted when Nathan was born in November of 1975.

My first experience with serious emotional problems was a year later, following a physical illness which almost took my life. The doctors were bewildered as to the cause and put me in quarantine for several days, eventually concluding only that the illness was viral. My digestive symptoms persisted for several months, and I lost weight until I looked like a skeleton. This experience seemed to permanently weaken my digestive system and set the stage for me to be overly anxious any time I would have similar symptoms in the future.

During these months I began to experience episodes of acute anxiety and some depression symptoms, though I did not know how to verbalize what I felt. The physicians did not seem well-versed in depression, anxiety, or panic, so these words were never mentioned to me. I simply knew that something was dreadfully wrong. Thinking that my body might have become depleted of nutrients, I loaded up on nutritional supplements, but to no avail. Though Nathan was the joy of my life, taking care of him was difficult during this time.

When I became pregnant with Seth, all of my physical and emotional symptoms vanished. I think this was probably due to a combination of hormonal changes and positive expectations. There was a reassuring normalcy about being pregnant. The doctor said the pregnancy would be high-risk due to my being under-weight, but I had no problems at all. Baby Seth, born the day before Easter in 1978, was small but healthy.

In the months after Seth's birth, I experienced a few brief spells (minutes long) of unexplained, moderate anxiety and a sense of unreality. Otherwise, I was a proud and happy mama, contentedly enjoying both of my sons.

Following John's graduation from seminary, we moved back to southern Illinois, a less exciting place, but a setting where we felt a sense of belonging. John and I enjoyed our family and the two congregations he was pastoring. During our three years in that pastorate, my only disconcerting experiences were: a slow recovery from an intestinal virus (and the accompanying anxiety); a few repetitions of the apparent separation anxiety; and some panic immediately before and during a plane flight to the Holy Land.

Let's pause here.

What red flags did you observe in my life story? For one thing, my nervous system seems to have always been overly sensitive or reactive. Also, I was easily conditioned in a negative way, i.e., one bad experience seemed to train me to react negatively in the future. Other than this, most of my problems were due to extremes: I was too afraid of pain and failure, so much so that I avoided some good situations and missed those opportunities to develop competence and confidence; I took life and myself too seriously, worrying too much, being too hard on myself, and taking things too personally.

What strengths or positives did you see that could serve me well later on, in my recovery? There were people and causes that mattered to me and motivated me. I enjoyed learning and accomplishing things; I was conscientious; I demonstrated determination and resolve and could persevere against the odds. I had experienced life as worthwhile and good for the most part. I had relationships with God and with caring people.

Chances are you have just as many assets or even more. Consider what strengths you have as a person, and what things you have going for you in your social, work, spiritual, recreational, financial, educational, or family settings. You do bring something positive to your own recovery; try not to let how you feel right now keep you from seeing this. If you draw a blank, ask someone who knows you to help you make a list of the positives. Or set about choosing to develop some strengths of your own. You do have some control, with God's help, over who you are, what you do, the influences to which you subject yourself, and the resources you access.

In any case, **recall the Bible story in which Jesus fed thousands with only a few loaves and fishes. You do not have to bring an impressive array of goodies to recovery; God can work with whatever you have to offer.**

Now back to the story:

In 1981 John and I moved to a larger community where John pastored one church, and again we were basically content. The worst of my personal difficulties, nameless and vague as they were to me, seemed to be in the past. Until…

Chapter 2

I Can Figure This Out!

1984.

I can't tell you exactly when I became sick. I think that John and his parents, who lived nearby, would say the first part of that year, possibly earlier. My mother thinks my problems began with the birth of my third son, Joseph, in December of 1982.

This is possible, because while I was in the hospital after the birth, I experienced undue anxiety over some minor breathing problems (related to the general anesthetic for my emergency C-section). Then after I went home, I was highly anxious about my post-partum bleeding, which was actually no more profuse than after the previous two deliveries. My mom, who came to help out for a few days, remembers that I "yelled a lot" at Nathan and Seth.

She returned home to Arkansas (she had moved back there in 1974 with Sarah and David), while we spent several weeks trying to soothe a colicky Joseph. My anxiety passed, but I was short on sleep. John helped a great deal during these first few weeks and then returned to his many outside activities.

I was not aware of feeling depressed, though I did feel overwhelmed and somewhat resentful that John was busy being Mr. Community when I still could have used more help at home. As a pastor, John had always been able to be home more than most dads, and he had been very involved in parenting, but I remember a few months when I believed he wasn't as sensitive to our needs as he might have been. Yet I enjoyed Joseph and his brothers and have many happy memories and prized photos from this time.

24

In May of 1984, John, Joseph, and I made a trip to Baltimore with John's parents for an international denominational gathering. It was an inspiring and enjoyable trip, but I nearly spoiled it for all of us with one instance of extreme anger.

I had been feeling weary, put-upon, and unappreciated. I know now that many depressions manifest this way. While on this trip I suddenly realized that some major expectations were about to fall squarely on my shoulders, and I wasn't sure I could handle them. I threw a fit that is embarrassing to recall.

A dark summer.

Another intestinal virus landed me in the hospital the night we arrived home from our trip. I spent Mother's Day partly wishing I was home with my kids and partly enjoying the break. Again my body did not recover quickly. All summer I had one digestive problem after another. My family physician ran tests and, as years earlier with different doctors, he found nothing.

Nathan and Seth remember that I was constantly scolding or punishing them that summer. They were fantastic kids but a good example of one plus one making three, and I definitely had a short fuse. Only later did I realize how cranky I had been. John's fears that my irritability had ruined the boys for life were unwarranted, but he couldn't have known that then.

I was miserable. I had problems falling asleep and staying asleep, and I awoke too early. I had less and less energy, and I began to lie around during the day in an attempt to get rested. I tried to rally for phone calls or when a family member needed me, but I was so lethargic. I spent more time in my nightgown and less time trying to look presentable. I went fewer places. The bed was my haven, though I never arose feeling rested.

In fact, nothing seemed to make any difference in how I felt. I experimented with what, when, and how I was eating. I tried changes in routine. Cut-backs in activities decreased the demands on me but changed little else.

Do you find that you have become very finicky, as I did? Though I became careless in some things, such as grooming and housecleaning, I became extremely picky in other things. The wrong food upset my colon; nausea and jitters developed if I didn't eat often enough. I avoided certain activities, such as driving, because I felt so strange. I could only sleep in certain positions.

If this describes you, both you and your loved ones are feeling frustrated, because having to do things "just so" is not making any long-term difference. These band-aid cures only make it possible for you to stay afloat.

The doctor put me on a mild tranquilizer in the summer of 1984, saying that my problem appeared to be "nerves." He told me he hoped I "would get on top of this soon" because these particular pills were habit-forming. I added this concern to my worry list, which was already long due to my discomfort and sense of helplessness. I also feared losing too much weight as I had in 1978, only this time pregnancy could not be a solution.

On our traditional family camping trip, which I had always enjoyed in the past, I spent the first night wringing my hands, crying, and trying not to throw up. I felt still worse in the morning, so we changed plans. John dropped me off at my mom and stepdad's place in Arkansas, then he took the boys camping and fishing. I felt guilty, helpless, and totally perplexed.

A small but significant realization.

Back at home, a little light dawned for me as I ate supper one evening. As usual I was struggling to choke down my food. John offered to pick me up some fast food if I thought I could eat it more easily and to take the boys to a friend's house, so that I could eat in peace. It was worth a try. While he was getting my food, I took an Ativan which did enable me to eat.

I sat at the table alone, chewing and reasoning, "I don't want to stay on this pill forever. Apparently I am capable of feeling relaxed and eating normally, because with one little pill I can manage it. **What I've got to do is figure out how to do for myself what this pill is doing for me.** I wonder how to do that." Though I did not see any solutions immediately, this conclusion was important. **I was coming closer to recognizing that the needed changes might be mostly internal and more than skin-deep.**

A darker fall.

Nathan and Seth began another school year, and I continued to worsen. I made three trips to a counselor who worked with pastors and their families. He thought it was significant that the word I used most to describe myself in our talks was "empty." I was referring to an empty stomach, but he believed I had a greater emptiness. I could see a million things in the Rorschach inkblots and gave such compulsively detailed answers that we only made it through a few cards. John, who was also frustrated and weary, was disappointed that these appointments didn't help me more. Later, when I was in the hospital, the counselor told John that he hadn't realized how serious my condition was.

At home I sat in a rocker and continued to try to analyze the situation. The thoughts that ran through my head repeatedly were, "I am just not myself," and "If anyone else asks me to do anything else, I am going to explode." I was not doing much at that point, but still felt over-burdened. I had nothing left to give.

If you are like I was, you have tried to figure this thing out. You keep thinking that if you find the cause, you can devise a solution. You experiment with things that you think will help. And you reflect and ruminate on your experience. You are trying to be a part of the solution, to return to normal living and your normal self.

However, in the process you may have become pre-occupied and self-absorbed. This was never your intention, but you may be in your own little world now. If you are also ex-pecting a great deal from others, you may appear selfish and insensitive. I don't say this to heap shame on you, but to help you grasp the reality of your situation. **If this shoe fits and you are not getting any help, it is time to accept some; otherwise you could become somebody you don't want to be.**

Here is a word picture that may depict where you are right now. When a contact lens-wearer loses a lens, she stands still and looks around, possibly squatting down and gingerly searching around her feet. However, she has trouble finding the lens because that which she needs in order to find it (her sight) is that which has been impaired by the loss. **You cannot see how to fix your mind because your mental capacity is compromised. That's why it may be necessary to accept input from someone else.**

Another thing you may experience is a sense of powerlessness, because so far nothing you have tried is making much difference. It's even possible that a situation beyond your control is largely responsible for your being depressed in the first place. Now you feel stuck for sure.

In the movie *Groundhog Day,* Phil, the main character, is in a bowling alley commiserating with a couple of other bowlers, and he says, **"What would you do if you were stuck in the same place, every day was the same, and nothing you do matters?"**

If you are very depressed, you probably can identify with such despair, in spite of blessings in your life.

One Sunday morning in October 1984, I skipped church (a more frequent occurrence all the time). Something had to give. I couldn't keep this up, and I was not being fair to John. I sat at our piano, playing hymns and weeping, and I said, "Lord, I give up. I've tried everything I know to try. I'm out of ideas. I don't know what's wrong here or what to do about it. **It's up to you. I give up.**"

Chapter 3

It Must Be Stress

Things happened fairly quickly after this. I believe **God took over when I gave up, though** there would not be any obvious improvement for quite some time. I think that sometimes God allows a situation to become absolutely critical so that both the urgency and the true problem are more obvious and we will get the proper help more readily. Also, we usually are more aware of our dependence on Him in such a crisis and therefore more willing to trust Him and to give Him the credit for change.

By mid-October my to-do list was down to laundry and helping the kids with their homework. I didn't do anything else or go anywhere. I had lost interest in almost everything, including sex, a noticeable contrast for me. This hadn't happened overnight either but was not like me at all.

Perhaps a break will do the trick.

In one last-ditch effort to rescue both myself and John, I spent a few days at my mother's. Our rationale was that perhaps my problem was stress, and getting away from all the things that tugged at me might provide some relief.

A thunderstorm overtook us on the way to my mom's, and I was unusually frightened by it. I felt so near the edge that I wasn't sure I could handle anything going wrong, even if it was just heavy rains. Of course, in that fearful, negative frame of mind, I imagined that a tornado would be just my luck.

Mama says that throughout my stay with her and Joe (my stepdad), I never seemed "crazy" (I had wondered), but I did seem nervous. I couldn't sit still for very long, so traveling in the car was difficult. I carried a cool washcloth with me for my forehead, as I had been doing for some time. I think this was a holdover from my childhood when this little trick helped calm an upset stomach or cool a fever. I lay around and tried to eat every couple of hours because I became weak and trembly if I didn't. I could never eat much at once and therefore felt empty again right away.

I think Mama and Joe suspected that my problems were partly psychological, because he had a talk with me one day in which he asked me if I needed some new goals at this time in my life. However, we were all confused as to the true nature of my condition because it appeared that something was physically wrong with me. Now I know that **depression and/or anxiety can cause almost every physical symptom in the book**. If you are just now coming to grips with the possibility that your own problems are psychological and not physical, get to a psychiatrist, psychologist, or counselor right away. You don't have to deteriorate as I did.

Then I came down with pneumonia, the fast-developing kind. The difficulty in breathing fostered new anxiety, and the heavy antibiotics created new symptoms. I was homesick and I felt even more guilty, because now I had to stay put until I could whip the pneumonia.

In an attempt to self-diagnose, I decided I was on too much medication, so I dropped the tranquilizer all at once. Big mistake. Now I could not sleep at all. I felt spacy. Nothing seemed real.

One night Mama, Joe, and I viewed a collection of family slides, something which I normally would have enjoyed. In the span of an hour or two, the entire lives of more than one generation passed before my eyes. I found myself thinking, "Is this all there is?" I felt panicky and left the room to catch my breath.

This reaction was not typical for me, so at breakfast the next morning I shared my experience with the two of them. They suggested I see a psychiatrist in Ft. Smith, and I agreed. A nurse for the physician who was treating my pneumonia secured me an appointment with the psychiatrist. The nurse was stunned at how soon she was able to get me in; I think God was working.

Does this sound like you?

Dr. Jacobs, the psychiatrist, was with me only a short time, because it didn't take long for a trained person to see what was going on. He showed me the *DSM-III* diagnostic criteria for both depression and panic disorder and asked, "Does this sound like you?" I recognized the panic disorder more quickly than the depression. He said that **anxiety disorders are a "What if" disease and I should stop thinking about all the things that could go wrong** (such as tornadoes). He told me not to stop the Ativan suddenly. Too late. He suggested I resume the Ativan and wean off of it gradually. Because he had an additional degree in pharmacology, I took his advice.

I was relieved to have a name for my problems, but I would have felt more relieved if I hadn't been skeptical about the depression diagnosis. As I left the doctor's office, he assured me, "You will get well." I thought, "Yeah, right."

Depressive and anxiety disorders commonly occur together. I had not realized that. I assumed that if I was wound up with anxiety, I could not be depressed at the same time. The reasons the two are associated are both chemical (the same neurotransmitters are involved) and environmental (common external factors and thought patterns).

Dr. Jacobs told me that **since I didn't get sick overnight, I would not get well overnight,** and therefore I should see a doctor closer to home. He gave me the name of one, but John located

32

another, Dr. Mason, and contacted him. John must have painted an alarming picture, because Dr. Mason suggested that I become an inpatient. Actually, his rationale made sense, because Dr. Mason and the hospital were three hours from home, and my being on site would allow for a closer monitoring of my medication. Also, I could participate in an intensive, multi-modal program which would facilitate a more rapid improvement. I consented to the plan, and my mother drove me back to Illinois.

Can things get any worse?

I got home on a Friday and was to be admitted on Monday, November 5. I was beyond disguising how awful I felt, so I chose not to see the boys that weekend; I feared their reaction to my condition, so they stayed with John's parents. This decision was tougher than anybody could appreciate; I had just been away for two weeks and was preparing to leave for an undetermined period of time. I wanted to see the kids so bad it hurt, but I would not be able to convincingly dispel any concerns they might have. My appearance alone might have worried them.

You may have had similar experiences. The guilt weighs on you, and you feel like your heart is breaking. In my case, John believed that I made the wrong decision.

That Saturday I approached John, who was working on the car, and I told him how sorry I was that things had been abnormal for so long. I said that I knew he missed having my help and the love-making, and I would do everything I could to benefit from treatment so that life could return to normal when I came home.

John's response was, "And I want you to know that you have no family to come home to. If you want to have a family again, you will have to earn one. You'll have to make a place for yourself in this family." I reeled at his coldness. I knew that he was worried and over-worked, but this I did not expect.

33

I tried to understand where he was coming from. He needed a break and some hope. He needed me to carry my share of the load and not lean on him so much. I understood his desperation for a major change, but how I wished he could have expressed himself some other way. If only he could have said something like, "I'm really glad to hear your intentions, because we can't take much more. We really need you to come home different." But he didn't say that. Any last vestiges of security within me vanished instantly. My anxiety skyrocketed, and my sense of shame deepened, at a point where I would have thought neither was possible.

Why is this important? Because now I had more to overcome. Another hurt. Another hurdle. Rejection and the fear of utter abandonment were piled on top of the rest. The work ahead of me was compounded. If John wanted to create a sense of urgency for me, he needn't have bothered. My own misery, my being away from the family, and my awareness that I wasn't pulling my weight were motivating enough. Possibly he did make me more aware of the family's investment in my recovery.

What John also accomplished accidentally was to sidetrack me. I had planned to concentrate on changing myself, and now it would take me a while to get re-focused, because I was preoccupied with my devastation and with thoughts of how to get him back.

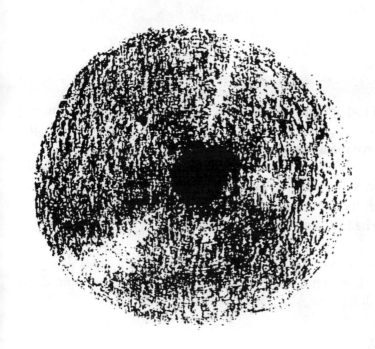

In a deep dark hole, crying out for help

How I was <u>before</u> I came to the hospital...

(expressive therapy - first week:
done in black crayon)

Chapter 4

This Can't Be Happening!

John had arranged for me to be admitted to St. Mark's through Dr. Mason, the chief of psychiatry who would also be my doctor. John drove me to the hospital, and I admitted myself. He told me he appreciated my doing this since he knew it took courage. His words were encouraging but did not begin to undo the heartache I felt from his previous remarks. He returned home to the boys, who we had agreed should be his priority.

The only thing I remember about admission besides doing the paperwork is that a chest X-ray was ordered to determine if my lungs still had traces of pneumonia; they did not.

Lock-up.

St. Mark's had three psych units at that time: an "open" unit where patients could sign themselves out for a few hours at a time; an intermediate ward; and lock-up. I was put in lock-up as a precautionary measure, because the doctor had not been able to assess suicide risk face-to-face; he had spoken with John over the phone but had not yet met or spoken with me.

The staff was kind but firm. They took away every personal possession, not just the dangerous-looking items, and gave me a hospital gown. The room was furnished with only a bed, an empty nightstand (which remained empty because I had nothing to put in it), and a dim, non-breakable wall mirror. My mother, who had also accompanied us to the hospital, stayed with me for a couple of hours. There was no chair for either of us to sit in. I have never felt like such a non-person in my life. There didn't seem to be much of the real me left anyway, and having all my privileges and belongings taken away was dehumanizing. The whole atmosphere had a Twilight Zone quality to it.

Lock-up had a small sitting room where other patients were gathered. Mama and I joined them. This room had a telephone, and it rang. A patient picked up the receiver and said, "Funny farm." In spite of my numbness, I was able to appreciate his sense of humor. Even in lock-up, I thought, there are some signs of life.

Transferred.

I had been given the last available bed in the locked unit. After a few hours, a new patient came in who was clearly in need of lock-up, so she was given my room. My clothes and purse were returned to me, and I was moved to the intermediate unit, which was also locked. I was relieved at first since I could keep some of my stuff with me, but the location of the new unit somehow seemed to be "farther back" in the hospital. I felt as if I were in a horror movie, being relegated to the back wards from whence I would never return. My mother had left earlier and I thought, "I am going to be lost here for sure, and nobody will know or care."

Somewhere in the course of the evening I was informed that Dr. Mason wanted to start me on an antidepressant and to take me off the Ativan - no weaning process, just cold turkey, the very thing Dr. Jacobs had advised me not to do. I was worried about this, and I do believe that my mental "spaciness" over the next few days was partly attributable to the withdrawal, though the strangeness of my surroundings also played a big part.

This ward was teeming with adolescents half my age. I was put into a room for two which already had two teenagers in it. My bed was rolled into the middle of the room. It was late at night by this time, and I wanted to try to sleep. However, the girls were highly agitated about having "the bitch" in the room,

37

and, speaking to each other as if I were not present, they threatened to kill me during the night. I really didn't think death was imminent, but neither was sleep under these circumstances, so I reported the goings-on to the nurse.

She moved my bed to a small, suffocating sitting room. This was the room used for small-group discussions and videos during the day. It smelled smoky (smoking was still allowed inside in 1984) and had no bathroom. When I needed a restroom in the night, I crossed the hall and asked the nurse where I should go. She said I would just have to hold it, because the only available bathroom was for staff only, behind the nurses' station, and I was not allowed to use it. Little incidents like this were so humiliating. Apparently my need to urinate was not legitimate. I persevered though, and another nurse relented, so I was allowed to use their toilet with a nurse standing there watching.

Morning came and I joined the other patients for breakfast in a larger room. I was the new person on the block, and nobody sought me out for company. However, when I joined a patient at her table, she was cordial. That was a pleasant change.

Transferred again.

I guess this staff concluded, as the lock-up staff had, that I posed no danger to myself or anyone else, because I was moved to the open unit that same morning. Its entrance was perpendicular to the secured doors of lock-up; we had passed it on the previous night. As I returned to this familiar-looking passage, I felt a little less removed from civilization. I was taken to room 558, my home for the next five weeks and a day.

Setting goals.

A nurse named Sharon sat beside me on the bed and explained that I would be participating in the Comprehensive Treatment

Unit, or CTU, program. We discussed how long I might be in the hospital. She handed me a form and asked me to write down a couple of goals and steps for reaching them. This would give some direction to my stay. I had a hard time with this. I knew I wanted to feel better, but I was supposed to put something more specific and measurable.

I saved the folder from CTU along with my forms and homework, all of which I still have. My initial goal sheet reads:

> **GOAL #1:** To do housework and care for Joseph at a normal energy level one week after I am home. **STEPS I NEED TO TAKE TO REACH THIS GOAL:** Control anxiety. Get more rest. Concentrate on positive thoughts and activities.
>
> **GOAL #2:** To be home by Thanksgiving. **STEPS I NEED TO TAKE TO REACH THIS GOAL:** Talk about self and anxieties, especially without getting anxious and down.
>
> **THINGS THAT KEEP ME FROM REACHING MY GOALS:** Thinking "What if." Impatience. Fearing inability to perform. No time to talk with John.
>
> **THOUGHTS I HAVE:** Wish I had time to talk to John.
>
> **HOW DO I CHANGE THIS:** Talk to John. Take sleeping pill. Make list to talk about.

I had added a note at the bottom of the page: "Assume responsibility at slow pace."

As you can see, I was feeling a painful lack of resolution with John. Also, I had no idea how to overcome the "things that keep me from reaching my goals."

If you are focused on not feeling bad anymore, you may be like I was. When people are miserable or in conflict, they are preoccupied with how they DON'T want things to be - with whatever it is they want to go away. **Switching the focus to how you DO want things to be and specifically how to accomplish this can be challenging. However, I encourage you to do this.**

When Joe had asked me about goals, he was on the right track, even though I could not see this at the time. In therapy or recovery, how will you know if you have reached your destination if you don't know what it is? I know it is difficult to see the long-term picture when you are just trying to hang on through the next hour, but it is important to try anyway. **Lack of direction is a stumbling block.**

Ask yourself what your priorities are; where you want to be in one, five, or ten years; what kind of person you want to be; how exactly you do want to function; which activities are worth doing. At this time, **it is more constructive to focus on these things than on how you want to feel**; I will explain this more later.

Ask yourself "what-would-it-take" questions. **"For me to get from here to there, what would it take?"** You may have to break this down into very small steps for now. A step towards your goals might involve washing the dishes or writing one short note to someone. Or just finishing this chapter. And then, **if you take a step, allow yourself to experience satisfaction with this progress**. Recovery begins with baby steps and occasional bursts of insight; you cannot fast-forward to the end.

Sizing up the problem.

I was administered the MMPI, a personality inventory which also assesses problem areas. I remember responding as honestly as I could, because I knew that someone was going to need an accurate picture of what was going on if they were going to help me. Even though I always harbored doubts that I would get better, I was desperate for help and I wanted to be taken seriously.

The interpretation of my MMPI results referred to a number of personal strengths. For example, the interpreter described me as "a trusting person who usually assumes the best about others." He wrote, "She behaves in an honest, straight-forward manner, and assumes that others will do likewise."

However, the interpretation also included the following commentary on my problems, which I hope will open a window into various aspects of your condition and also provide some checkpoints against which you can measure my progress and yours:

> This patient is….. not at all insightful about herself, her own role in things. She is not psychologically-minded. She does, however, have a high sense of social responsibility, but represses her own motives and drives.
>
> She is depressed, but it appears to be atypical. She may even at times be seen smiling through her tears. It is as though emotion is about to well up in her and she is about to pour forth with all sorts of talk and feelings and obvious emotions, but at the same time she tries to deny that this is going on. She barely admits that she is depressed but does admit freely to anxiety. She seems "bottled up" with emotion and has a great deal of need to ventilate these pressures and feeling.
>
> There is considerable free-floating anxiety with tension and nervousness expressing itself largely through her autonomic nervous system, and she might expect such symptoms as tachycardia, muscle tension, headaches, chest pains, perhaps hypertension and various gastro-intestinal disturbances with restlessness, insomnia and a frequent sense of dread.

She is somewhat reserved and shy in her social interactions. She dislikes being the center of attention and she feels uncomfortable at parties or in crowds. She is inhibited, easily embarrassed and somewhat isolated.

She experiences fears which may cause discomfort in her daily life or even constriction of her activities. This unrealistic fear of such things as heights, fire, storms and injury suggests a phobic reaction to chronic or acute anxiety.

She tends to be passive and complaining. She does not recognize or accept her own role in what is going on. She sits back passively and expects other people to do things for her, take care of her, love her, etc. and when they don't do enough, she whines and complains.

She is very adverse to taking any kind of risk. She is very conservative. She does not wish to have anything to stir up any more anxiety even if it's for fun.

Not a very flattering commentary but mostly true. I felt insulted by the suggestion that I did not have much insight into myself, and I would have liked for someone to understand that the passivity was partly an attempt to become rested from the ever-present fatigue. However, the interpreter was more correct than I wanted to believe. I'm sure John would have agreed with his comments, because I had basically become a fourth child for him to take care of.

The consultant goes on to recommend specific antidepressants and Alprazolam (Xanax), along with "ventilative therapy." He indicates that I "will need a long-term relationship where she has an interested, concerned listener."

Settling in for the long haul.

St. Mark's had hospitality suites where family members of

patients could stay. My mother stayed several days. There was not anything she could do for me, but she wanted me to have the satisfaction of knowing there was a caring, familiar person nearby. My home and friends were three hours away; the drive from her own home was about ten hours, too far to allow her to just drop by during visiting hours.

The staff had some concerns (about which they informed me much later) that Mama's presence might hinder my progress; they supposed I was too enmeshed with her or too dependent. I have considered whether they were right. I don't think I was too enmeshed. I did tend to be too dependent on others in general, because I had more confidence in other people than I did in myself, but frankly I did not lean on her much during this time, and she did not interfere with my participation in the program.

I wish I could say that I at least felt comforted by Mama's presence, but nothing made much difference in how I *felt*. Nothing could touch the terror and emptiness I felt inside. I did appreciate her consideration and the sacrifices she was making in being away from home. It never occurred to me to suggest that she return home sooner than she did. I was consumed with how bad I felt, and I didn't consider much else.

I sometimes met my mother for a meal in the hospital cafeteria, and during free time we took walks outside. Sidewalks provided a pathway through a flower garden and beyond to a hill with concrete benches. While I was trying to get acclimated, we familiarized ourselves with the hospital and its grounds.

CTU kept me busy most of my waking hours, except on weekends when we patients had more free time. Some of CTU's activities were required; some were optional. Our unit was a mixed bag - men, women, and adolescents, from depressed to delusional. Patients whose primary problems were eating disorders or addictions were located on a different wing.

I experienced a sense of unreality for several days. I felt disconnected. The situation seemed abnormal; I seemed abnormal, and it seemed to me that I was treated accordingly. I longed for the normal and familiar.

More than just a mental patient.

Early in my stay somebody put the rails up on my bed. I don't know why, but in my confused state, I assumed there was a good reason, so I left them up. Unknowingly I maintained some of my anxiety and "stuckness" by doing this. While it was important for me to acknowledge my mental illness and not be in denial, it was also important that I try to do everything as normally as possible. My self-image had become that of a helpless, ill person, and I unknowingly maintained that image when I kept the rails up. I had swallowed the "I admit I am sick" message thoroughly.

If you have been diagnosed with a disorder, don't be defensive about this; but on the other hand, do not allow yourself to believe that these symptoms and labels are the sum total of you. You are more than your illness! You may be sick, but this is not all you are.

A couple of weeks into my hospital stay, I looked at the rails and thought, "I don't need these stupid things." I lowered them and felt a release, as if I had broken free from something.

[Note: If you have considered inpatient treatment, please do not be deterred by my earliest experiences at St. Mark's. Overall, this intensive treatment program was what I needed, and I benefited immensely from it; if I had it to do over, I would go without hesitation. More alternatives exist now, e.g., explicitly Christ-centered programs such as the New Life Clinics and the Rapha Treatment Centers. So if I were considering inpatient treatment right now, I would probably look into one of these or something like it. However, I maintain that a program such as the one I was in is definitely worthwhile!]

Chapter 5

Why Won't They Believe Me?

In my first meeting with Dr. Mason, he briefed me on the things John had told him in their telephone conversation. In an attempt to ensure that the doctor understood my condition was serious, John had exaggerated to the point of lying. For example, he told Dr. Mason that I had not fed Joseph a single time during the first year of his life. I had breast-fed Joseph for a full twelve months, so that assertion made no sense. I know that John needed to have someone understand how much of the burden he had been carrying, but he did me a disservice here. Appropriate medical treatment must be based on the facts, yet Dr. Mason clearly was working with a distorted picture.

By the grace of God I did not slip completely over the edge, but this state of affairs tripped me up in more ways than one: I was angry with John for exaggerating, and I felt humiliated that the doctor was reluctant to believe me. When I tried to clarify the account, Dr. Mason said, "Who should I believe? After all, you are the patient." In other words, as a mental patient I had no credibility. My defensiveness and anxiety were raised another notch.

I understood that I had been behaving abnormally, and I had no intentions of communicating anything to the contrary, but the facts spoke for themselves without any embellishment. As with the MMPI, I knew that establishing my true condition was important, and I was thoroughly exasperated that I was not considered a reliable source in determining what that was.

In spite of my desire to continue explaining the facts until somebody believed me, I gave this up. The more I explained, the more upset I became, and the more agitated I was about

something, the less I was believed. So I chose to shut my mouth. Not until months later in an outpatient appointment did I attempt to broach the subject again; this time I was believed.

I found that the attitudes of the rest of the staff were similar to Dr. Mason's. They were not unkind, but neither were they warm, and they did not seem interested in hearing my account of anything, ironic since they were simultaneously urging me to open up and talk about whatever was on mind. I guess they were wanting me to **get in touch with deeper stuff such as repressed feelings, and quit trying to explain and defend**, but the lack of validation was hurtful to me.

A resolution.

I chose to cooperate, but I also resolved never to treat anybody the way I was being treated (or perceived I was being treated). From my present perspective as a counselor, **I can understand that I was being discouraged from having a pity party or going over the same old ground repeatedly, but I still believe that it would have been helpful to go over some of this ground one time with an open listener.** A lid was put on some significant matters at a time when I was supposed to be "venting." My need to be taken seriously and the dynamics between John and me were not just fringe issues; they merited attention. I guess the staff figured I would get started and not know when to stop.

I have kept my resolution in relating to my own clients. I try to avoid being patronizing, condescending, or demeaning in any way. **Being depressed or anxious is not the equivalent of being stupid and senseless.** I allow for the fact that a person's story may not exactly duplicate reality, but the client's perceptions still deserve respect and her feelings empathy, and I do not want her to feel discounted. I also explain things to her as if she has sense and the ability to grasp what I am saying, unless I

47

clearly observe the contrary. I try to offer warmth and encouragement without slipping into codependent caretaking or enabling. [Though I refer to "her," depression and anxiety are not confined to the female population.]

Is it possible that I was wrong about the staff's view of us? Of course, because everything was filtered through my own sense of shame. A later incident, though, confirms that perhaps they could have used an attitude adjustment. Several of us patients were trying to become better acquainted. One evening we were sitting around chatting, casually dressed because it was almost bedtime. Ann, one of the patients, wore her favorite floppy slippers and something comfortable but mismatched. Another patient joined us and informed us that as she passed by a group of nurses, she overheard them laughing and ridiculing Ann for how she was dressed. Ann cried, and we all understood. If she was being ridiculed, we probably were, too. (By the way, none of this group had any pathological paranoia that I was aware of.)

Caring takes many forms.

As far as whether any of the nurses or therapists really cared about us, I believe they did, even if they did not usually convey warmth. Chances are they were disgusted by a steady stream of poor-me attitudes; also they must have needed some degree of detachment in order to do such intense work day after day without being pulled down by it. In addition, if none of them had ever been where we were, they simply did not understand how it felt to be in our shoes.

This subject brings up a pertinent issue. **I had a deeply ingrained assumption that caring or concern can be measured by the amount of fretting or intensity demonstrated. That is, I believed that when I was upset, anyone who cared about me should be as upset as I was. I had to learn that a person can be concerned for you and even love**

48

you deeply without getting sucked into your crisis. I must set limits now with my own clients on how involved I can be in their turmoil and their lives, and I do not disintegrate in a session, even if they do. Does this mean I don't care? Not at all. It just means that I have learned where I end and they begin, and especially **I have learned that to get "worked up" about things over which I have no control is a terrible waste of emotional energy.**

If you have warm, empathetic listeners in your life, they can be a blessing. In fact, I encourage you to seek out such a listener. But if you do not find one, don't let this stop you from getting well. Perhaps your perceptions of others' views of you are incorrect or unfair. However, if others are in fact letting you down, belly-aching about it won't do any good, and definitely drop the need to hear others say that you are right. **Having someone believe in you and understand you 100% of the time is NOT necessary for you to get well.**

<u>**Picture a continuum**</u>.

I will close this chapter by sharing a concept presented in one of our groups. This was the idea of a mental health continuum, comparable to a physical health continuum. Most individuals fall in the middle rather than at the extreme poles, and **no definite line clearly distinguishes healthy from unhealthy, normal from abnormal. What this meant to me was that I was not in a separate category of human beings.** I was a person who happened to have specific problems, not a problem person, and definitely not a non-person. I found this understanding helpful.

49

Chapter 6

What If I Faint?

The side effects of medication and all my questions about various pills hampered my ability to follow the routine simply and calmly. I felt anything but calm; I felt "wired" and strange. As I said earlier, stopping the Ativan suddenly may have contributed to that feeling.

Side effects.

The first antidepressant caused such drops in my blood pressure that I could barely function, so Dr. Mason started me on Elavil. I had the same reaction to this, but he insisted that I **tough it out, because most antidepressants would probably have the same effect and we would waste our time experimenting.** He also believed Elavil would help me sleep, which it did.

I would awake in the mornings feeling drugged, but at least I did not spend half the night tossing and turning. I occasionally woke up in the night feeling tingly all over, especially on my scalp, and I assumed this was from the Elavil. The biggest problem was the light-headedness I felt upon waking. Raising my head off the pillow made everything go black.

One night I awoke in the wee hours because I needed to use the bathroom, but there was no way I could get there, because I was too lightheaded to get out of bed. I rang for the nurse, who brought me a bed pan. As I tried to slide it under me, I struggled to stay conscious. I was almost too dizzy to stay upright while I took care of the matter. I was "with it" just enough to feel humiliated that two nurses stood at the foot of the bed while I used the bed pan. They looked at me as if to say, "Boy, is she in bad shape." They may have understood what was going on, but I imagined they had been told that I was too dependent and saw my appeal as an unnecessary helplessness. In reality, I would have given anything to have slipped into and out of the bathroom on my own. I shed a few tears, then, thanks to the Elavil, I went right back to sleep.

The same dizziness was a problem each morning when I awoke to start my day. Later in the day I felt faint each time I stood up because my blood pressure shifted (an orthostatic drop). The nurses checked my blood pressure and pulse several times a day in the beginning, as they did for all the patients. Later they did this less often. Typically Sharon stood beside me with her fingers on my wrist and said, "High as usual."

My hands became very shaky from the Elavil. Some of my written assignments are difficult to read because I could not hold the pen steady. I remember that when the shakiness was at its worst, I had difficulty eating. One night I sat in the patient dining room feeling embarrassed that I could not get my food to my mouth. With dogged determination I used both hands and managed to get a few bites to my mouth with a spoon. This side effect went away after a few weeks.

The Elavil made my mouth as dry as cotton, so I carried water with me everywhere. Tricyclic antidepressants like Elavil can dry out the whole system, so I also became constipated.

One nurse advised me, "Drink coffee. That'll help." Another nurse said, "Whatever you do, don't drink coffee."

So I requested a stool softener, which caused torrents of diarrhea, and you can guess what that did to my anxiety level, considering my history. During a twenty-four hour period the nurses called Dr. Mason twice for me, first about the constipation, then about the diarrhea. The nurse who talked to

51

him the second time said that he was disgusted with me and wanted me to **start taking things better in stride**. Fortunately, the diarrhea ended as abruptly as it began, and I was no worse for wear. For the time being, I took no more stool softeners.

A peculiar symptom which I supposed was a side-effect was the urgent sensation that I need to urinate and would not be able to control this function. This urge hit me hardest one day when I was taking a break with my mother. We had gone to a mall, and instead of being able to enjoy the Christmas decorations, all I could think about was locating the restrooms. To my surprise, I never did lose control of my bladder. As an aside, Mama remembers that when we stepped into an elevator that day and the doors closed, I freaked and said, "I've got to get out of here," so we got out the first time the doors opened. I had forgotten this.

More questions.

I worried quite a bit about medication. Would it be effective? How long would it take? Would I be able to hang on that long? Would I get hooked? Did taking medication make me a moral or spiritual failure? As a Christian, shouldn't I be able to do this on my own? After all, at my own supper table I had wished for a way to recover without depending on pills. Would that be possible?

I always had the option to refuse to take the medication, and sometimes I wavered as to whether I really wanted to swallow a pill. The nurse would hold the pill in her extended hand, and I would hesitate a long time. Still, I did not have many alternatives, and even though no one could guarantee I would feel better with the pill, no one could guarantee that without it, either.

The doctor told me that he thought my depression was at least partly chemical, so the chances were good that medication would help. Once the neurotransmitters were

balanced and stabilized for a while, I would be able to omit the pills. Learning healthy coping skills would also decrease the chances of my becoming dependent on medication.

Elavil was not addictive. Xanax, (brand name for Alprazolam, an anti-anxiety drug) could be, and once I learned this, I avoided taking it except in emergencies. It was ordered for me to take only "as needed" anyway. Many people do take Xanax regularly without any negative consequences, but I was cautious.

I was a typical anxiety patient in my worries about the pills. I have observed that my clients with significant anxiety are the same ones who are most likely to worry about medication and mostly likely to be "sensitive" to it. I am not certain how much of this sensitivity is chemical and how much is caused by worry, but these individuals are likely to want their pills scored to be cut in half, so they can take small or personally-tailored doses. They also are prone to question their doctor's judgment about medication and to purchase books about prescription drugs so they can do their own research. I was like that.

The waiting game.

As I continued to develop new symptoms during my first few days in St. Mark's, I wondered if they represented a worsening of my condition (since the Elavil had not kicked in yet) or a negative reaction to the medication. For example, I experienced more frequent and intense panic attacks. I should have spoken more freely with the doctor about this, but to talk about these things seemed like complaining (or not taking things in stride), so I mostly kept my concerns to myself.

If you have begun taking psychotropic meds, you may need someone to sympathize with how long the wait is for positive change. I was told more than once that I might feel better in just three weeks. At that distress level, the words "just" and "three weeks" don't go together. At times my inner torment was so excruciating that I wondered how I would survive the next five minutes. Three weeks-----PFFFT.

Some of the newer antidepressants work faster, but the long wait is a fact of life. Try to be patient and use your time focusing on measures over which you have more control. Drugs like Xanax work faster - in and out like aspirin - and your doctor may give you something like this to take during acute episodes, especially while you are in the waiting stretch.

If you are afraid that you will pass out at home and remain unconscious without being found, arrange for someone you trust to call or drop by daily at designated times for a week of two. Make a point either to be there or to let them know if you change plans. Agree on what they will do if you do not answer the phone or door. **A reliable plan can help to allay your fears.** Without a plan you may call an unreasonable number of people before the day is over.

If you have reactions to medication that suggest allergies or a threat to your life, or that truly make it impossible for you to function, then by all means tell your doctor. But in general, recognize that some discomfort may be inevitable before the drug becomes effective, and try increasing your tolerance for this discomfort. Unfortunately, the negative side effects usually kick in earlier than the benefits. When in doubt, talk to your doctor or pharmacist about your concerns, and then take seriously what they say. I have noticed that often people will do the former but not the latter. Yes, you know your own body, but no, you are not the doctor.

Some of the side effects will disappear as your body adjusts, and some will not. Later, after I went home, I used a stool softener as needed, with surprisingly good results. The blood pressure problem diminished. My dry mouth persisted as

54

long as I took Elavil, which was for at least three years. As I became stronger, I decreased the dosage, but I was on a high dose for a year or more. **Do not stop this kind of medication suddenly, unless the doctor orders it.**

While I was still in St. Mark's, **I figured out how to manage the low blood pressure.** Upon awakening, I would raise my feet and legs up in the air. This increased the blood flow to my head. As I felt less faint, I would elevate the head of my bed. Then I gradually sat up and swung my feet off the side, sitting there a few minutes before standing.

"What a lot of trouble just to get out of bed," I thought. I resented having to go through this little ritual, but Dr. Mason reacted favorably when I told him about it, saying this was a **sign that I was being resourceful and not helpless.** He was right, of course, but I still felt inconvenienced.

No less a Christian.

I resolved my am-I-less-a-Christian issues by accepting that taking pills for my illness was no different from taking antibiotics for an infection or insulin for diabetes. I could readily accept that God uses doctors and medical treatments for physical problems. If my disturbances were partly chemical in origin, then they, too, were "physical" to some degree.

I learned later that the Christian psychiatrists Frank Minirth and Paul Meier maintain that depression, if it lasts long enough, can cause changes in the electrochemistry of the brain. That is, **depression can both be caused by, and in turn cause further, chemical changes that work against the person. Medication helps to reverse the problem.**

If you can't take medication...

If the first medication you try simply doesn't work, or is more trouble than it's worth, don't be afraid to try another. Your doctor may be able to find something which better fits your needs and also avoids the side-effects that trouble you most. It may take some experimentation to find what works best for you. More alternatives are available now than in 1984.

However, some individuals never do find an antidepressant that they can take safely or comfortably. If this describes you, take heart. Medication is not the only alternative, nor is it a necessary adjunct for most people who are wanting to benefit from psychotherapy.

In fact, the evidence from well-controlled studies indicates that cognitive-behavior therapy is at least as effective as medication – even in the case of severe depression – for both the short term and the long term (Antonuccio, Danton, and DeNelsky, 1995). Furthermore, one study showed that over a two-year period, cognitive-behavior therapy was more cost-effective than medication (Antonuccio, Thomas, and Danton, 1997). **So if you cannot take antidepressants, find a cognitive-behavior therapist and/or read and apply some books that present this approach in a practical manner (I will explain this kind of therapy and refer to specific titles on the subject in a later chapter).**

In light of the possiblity of recovery without medication, why would anyone want to take pills, with their side effects and expense? I did not suggest that antidepressants are ineffective – only that some people can't take them and others may not need them. Drugs' usefulness lies in their ability to bring about more immediate symptom relief for certain individuals and to be especially helpful for depressions that are primarily chemical in origin. Also, because a high level of internal distress can result in suicide, medication may help to save lives by reducing the distress.

I think that the Elavil facilitated and enhanced the usefulness of CTU for me, by reducing the symptoms that were distracting me and by increasing my ability to concentrate on and assimilate the program's various components. Some research does suggest that I was not unusual, i.e., that in the case of *severely* depressed patients, the combination of psychotherapy and drugs is more effective than psychotherapy alone (Barchas, Marzuk, and Siegel, 1998), though these results have not been replicated as many times as those quoted earlier.

Could I have progressed without the Elavil? Probably, but I don't like to think about how much lower I might have sunk first.

Detoured from my original goal.

What became of my earlier determination to do for myself what the pills were doing for me? I never lost this resolve; it would just take longer than I expected to arrive at a place where non-medical measures alone would be enough.

Chapter 7

If I Were a Fit Mother....

Guilt threatened to consume me – guilty feelings, that is. I agonized over the prospect that my kids might be feeling abandoned. I longed for a chance to reassure them that I loved them and to explain why I was away from home. As in years past, I hated thinking that I had left someone hurting or that they might be thinking badly of me. On top of this, Nathan's ninth birthday was celebrated without me (the first week I was in St. Mark's). Did he understand where his mom was on his special day?

I was a Christian, a wife, a pastor's wife for that matter, a mother, and a college graduate. What was I doing here? This felt like prison, so did this mean I had committed a crime? Knowing that I was not actually locked in did not alleviate my feelings of being trapped and imprisoned and completely at the mercy of other people.

In an attempt to perk myself up, I took a walk around the building and found myself looking in the windows of the baby nursery. The infants were so sweet, and I was reminded of my own boys as newborns. Sentimental, poignant feelings swept over me. I missed my sons. I walked away feeling even more guilty for being separated from them.

For the first week, I sat in group only partially listening, because I kept thinking, "What kind of mother am I to be in this place? I am not where I'm supposed to be." I wondered if I was wasting my time.

One day I sat in our circle, feeling panicky and nauseous, with sweat breaking out all over. I left the group and went to the restroom, where I bathed my face with wet paper towels and cried. I looked at myself in the mirror. I had no make-up on, and my broken glasses were taped together in the middle. I looked as horrible as I felt, and I didn't care. I begrudgingly rejoined the group, strictly from the realization that I had no where else to go.

As I mentioned earlier, I worsened emotionally and physically before I began to make improvement. A passage in the sixth chapter of Job describes how I felt:

> If only my anguish could be weighed and all my misery
> placed on the scales! It would surely outweigh the sand of the
> seas..... What strength do I have, that I should still hope? What
> prospects, that I should be patient? Do I have the strength of
> stone? Is my flesh bronze? Do I have any power to help myself?
> (verses 2-3a, 11-13a)

I cannot say that at this point I had much faith in God. My faith had been rattled, and only later would it be restored. For now I felt like Phil in *Groundhog Day*, who gives this internal weather report to Rita and Larry: "It's gonna be cold, it's gonna be gray, and it's gonna last you the rest of your life."

As I became acquainted with the other patients, I learned that several of them had been in CTU for weeks already. One woman had spent almost three months there and was apprehensive about her imminent discharge. A number of people had been hospitalized for treatment in the past. I found this discouraging and frightening. I wondered if a lifetime of institutionalization was what I had ahead of me. Such thoughts produced a knot in my stomach, but they also increased my determination to benefit as much as possible this time around so that I would never need to return. I propped up photos of my three sons on the window ledge as an additional motivator, though every time I looked at them I winced from feelings of sadness and guilt.

Clearing the hurdle.

I crossed the guilt hurdle by refusing to think guilt-inducing thoughts. I reminded myself that I was doing the right thing seeking treatment and that I would be a better wife and mother for having recovered. At that time, I could not have gone home and carried out normal responsibilities in a normal way. This program was necessary.

There is a saying prominent in twelve-step recovery programs that goes something like this: **if you keep on doing what you've been doing, you'll keep on getting what you've been getting.** Going home and blindly trying again would have been no more fruitful than it was before. So I chose to be positive about this option, and I tried to focus on the program.

Guilty feelings vs. actual guilt.

Many of the emotions and moods that go with depression do not mean anything. By that, I mean that **you should not assume that everything you feel is grounded in fact. Feeling guilty does not automatically mean that you are guilty.**

However, if your feelings of guilt seem to be the conviction of the Holy Spirit concerning actual guilt, then ask God to show you specifically what your sins are. Confess and repent before God and accept His forgiveness. He will forget your sins faster than most people will. If folks are judgmental of you, or you feel that Satan is trying to make you feel condemned, claim Romans 8:1: "Therefore, there is now no condemnation for those who are in Christ Jesus." Satan is the Accuser of the Brethren. Do not allow his voice to speak to you more loudly than God's. A vague, broad, persistent sense of condemnation is probably not from God and should not be accepted.

Mental patients and counseling clients are worthy of respect.

There is no shame either in needing help or in accepting it. My being in St. Mark's represented strength as much as weakness.

Scott Peck in *The Road Less Traveled* wrote, "**Entering psychotherapy is an act of the greatest courage**. The primary reason people do not undergo psychotherapy is not that they lack the money but that they lack the courage." Admitting to a problem, accepting help and scrutiny, and committing to change are challenges.

If you are reaching out, pat yourself on the back. If you are actively participating in your own therapy, hold your head high!

Chapter 8

You Don't Understand!

"What does he know, anyway?"

This question ran through my head numerous times about all the professionals who worked in CTU. **My thinking was that if a person did not completely understand where I was coming from, she or he could not possibly help me. My usual trust of people, referred to in the MMPI results, was compromised at this point.** Why was this a stumbling block? Because I could have benefited from the program earlier if I had trusted the staff more.

I cooperated in terms of participation; I didn't skip any therapy groups or educational activities, but I silently questioned their value. There's nothing wrong with being appropriately cautious or discerning, but I was too skeptical. I was saying, "I'm desperate! Help me, please!" and then responding, "But you don't understand!" when help was offered.

Though I carried the thought a bit too far, I did have a point. John Maxwell, a pastor in California, says, **"People don't care how much you know until they know how much you care."** When I was the patient, having a professional care about me in an understanding way would not only have felt good; it also would have enhanced my confidence in the program as a whole. Romans 12:15 tells us "to rejoice with those who rejoice and mourn with those who mourn." Having someone to mourn with me, without encouraging a pity party, would have fostered hope and confidence.

I believe Maxwell's philosophy and apply it wholeheartedly with my own counseling clients today. My caring about them increases their confidence in whatever hope and help I can offer.

God understands.

I believe God understands our turmoil, though I doubted this during my darkest hours. The Psalmist clearly struggled with some of the same hardships we do, and we have his written outpourings by God's design. Psalm 13 includes phrases like this:

> How long, O Lord? Will you forget me forever? How long will you hide your face from me? How long must I wrestle with my own thoughts and every day have sorrow in my heart?..... Look on me and answer, O Lord my God. Give light to my eyes, or I will sleep in death. (verses 1-3)

Or how about this:

> Hear my prayer, O Lord; let my cry for help come to you. Do not hide your face from me when I am in distress. Turn your ear to me; when I call, answer me quickly. For my days vanish like smoke; my bones burn like glowing embers. My heart is blighted and withered like grass; I forget to eat my food. Because of my loud groaning I am reduced to skin and bones. I am like a desert owl, like an owl among the ruins. I lie awake; I have become like a bird alone on a housetop..... My days are like the evening shadow; I wither away like grass. (Ps. 102: 1-7, 11)

The inclusion of such verses in God's Word tells me that He does understand. He validates our inner torment as legitimate.

I indicated in Chapter 5 that you may feel discredited, and you may not find anyone who seems to understand the full extent of your torment. What I am adding here is that you may even feel that the people you are looking to for help have NO window at all into how you really feel, that they are clueless and are content to stay that way.

So I reiterate, if you have someone who empathizes or "mourns" with you, be grateful, but if no one does this, **don't postpone recovery waiting for someone to come through for you**. It would be irrational for you to let yourself down just because you feel others are letting you down. And in the meantime, **remember that Jesus wept with Mary and Martha (Jn. 11:35) and is weeping with you, even if no one else seems to be**. God is our Comforter (2 Cor. 1:4) and the Holy Spirit our ever-present Counselor (Jn. 14:26), even if he doesn't have skin on.

Don't ignore the very people who may be God's answer to prayer.

While you are waiting for the perfect human helper, you run the risk of missing good things that are already coming your way. In my case, I was discounting helpful people just because I felt discounted. On one of the outdoor walks that I took with my mother, she said to me, **"Just think of the people you may be able to help because you've been through this."** I thought, "If she knew how bad off I really am, she wouldn't say that. Fat chance I'll ever be well enough to help anybody!" Because I didn't feel thoroughly understood, I disregarded her words of encouragement. Individuals may be sharing things with you that you truly need to hear. Don't blow them off just because you think they don't fully understand. God may be speaking to you through them.

How can you trust the professional, who may or may not demonstrate a deep empathy for your pain? **I gradually learned to trust my helpers by reminding myself of these three things: 1) they were trained in this field and had experience in it; 2) they might be God's answer to my prayers; and 3) their**

individual lives seemed to be in better shape than mine. They seemed to know something or do something that I did not know or do.

I do not believe that every mental health professional is an equally good match for every client, nor do I think it wise to go to the other extreme and be so skeptical of help that you dismiss a good resource when he or she is staring you in the face. Just as a physician can be effective in treating you medically without ever having had your particular ailment, other professionals can also be helpful without having experienced everything you have.

Nowhere to go but up.

On one of my lowest days, I received word of a patient who was being moved to a more restricted unit because she was suicidal. I looked out at the gray November skies and thought, "If this thing doesn't get turned around within a week, that's going to be me. I cannot take this much longer." Because I feared that I was reaching the limits of my endurance, I could understand why people consider suicide. Usually they don't want to be dead; they just need relief and see no other way to get it.

On a positive note:

The good news is this: I was on the road to recovery and just did not realize it. **Recovery does not begin when you feel better. Recovery begins with changes in your thoughts and your behavior, even your speech.**

I did two things that were significant in a positive way. The first is that when I had a panic attack, I began saying to myself, "This will pass. It always does." I did not understand then what causes such attacks, but I had noticed that they seemed to be self-limiting. Telling myself this almost brought me comfort; it definitely allowed me to begin to control my behavior.

Instead of running from the room, I sat still, focused on the group discussion, and reminded myself that the panic wasn't going to last forever.

The second positive step was putting on make-up one morning even though I didn't feel like it. As with the ritual for getting out of bed, I resented the effort this took, but I thought, "Why not? It's a normal thing to do." Dr. Mason complimented me on my appearance, which spurred me on.

In your own situation, try telling yourself something positive, factual, and relevant. **Look at the evidence – all the evidence – for your true condition. The evidence told me that the panic would pass and not destroy me.**

Also, try doing something normal in spite of how you feel. Then, if noone else gives you any positive reinforcement, give yourself some. Compliment yourself, or make a note in a journal, or reward yourself somehow. **Learning to do the right thing in spite of your feelings is vital to wellness.**

The simple suggestions above are typical of what is called cognitive-behavior therapy. This kind of psychotherapy is based on the premise that the best way to change your feelings and moods is to consciously and directly change your thoughts and behaviors first. Research demonstrates that this approach works, and it definitely worked for me, even though I didn't know what to call it at the time. Attempts to directly change your feelings are rarely productive. I was on the right track. It just took a while for my feelings to catch up.

I would never reach that suicidal point.

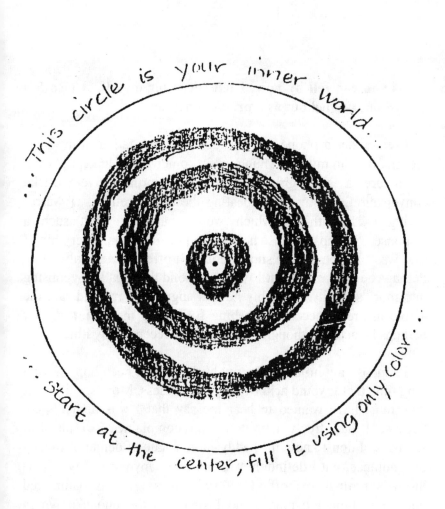

(expressive therapy - second week:
done in black & yellow)

Chapter 9

Why Pick On Me?

As you can tell by now, I felt sorry for myself. I also felt picked on, singled out as a problem person.

I remember a phone conversation with my father-in-law. For the first time in my life, I hung up on somebody. He kept saying, "You are a sick girl." He avoided normal give-and-take conversation, mostly just repeating the above refrain. I wasn't saying twisted things which would naturally elicit such a response. Perhaps because he regarded me as "sick," everything I said was suspect, and he simply couldn't offer me any validation. Perhaps he was afraid that I would respond to empathy by lapsing into more self-pity. Possibly he was angry with me and said the above in preference to unleashing something more hurtful. Or perhaps he actually thought I still had not accepted my illness.

I suppose my in-laws, like my husband, had been hoping for a long time that I would acknowledge my illness. More specifically, they must have wanted to hear me say that I was mentally ill, because I had freely admitted (and complained of) physical sickness. I don't know if I had been in a state of denial or mostly of ignorance, but I definitely was not there anymore. My father-in-law's timing was off. The "sick" message was hammered home one time too many, and I slammed the phone down in exasperation. Of course, I did not make myself look healthy when I did this, I'm sure.

Is everyone else off the hook?

I was exasperated not only by my in-laws' approach to me during my illness, but also by the bigger picture of which this was a part. I believe that John's family (with whom I generally had

68

more contact than with my own) had some misconceptions that caused them to view me not only with a natural consternation, but with an unnatural resentment or at least suspicion.

I acknowledge that I could be wrong, but here is how I see it: As a baby, John was nearly lost during a difficult pregnancy and delivery. That he was miraculously not lost seemed to have created in his family a special expectation that he should live a charmed life, i.e., that he should not only "go far" and be happy, but that everyone should make this easy and trouble-free. We may all wish this for our children, but we don't generally *expect* it. I think that because they had such high hopes for him, they were thrown for a loop by the hardships that came his way because of me. Though they normally were accepting, gracious people, they seemed to maintain and foster in John the idea that if I was making his life difficult, even unintentionally, then perhaps I wasn't supposed to be part of the picture.

Lest you think I am imagining this, here are a couple of things that were said to me later. During my first month home, my mother-in-law said, "I hope you realize that no man but John would have taken you back." And John himself said to me, "I will never believe that you were ill. You're just plain mean. I believe that your primary goal in life is to make the boys and me miserable, and nothing you can ever say or do will make me change my mind."

I do not share these things about John and his family to hurt them. I share them with you because **this is a book about stumbling blocks to recovery, and the attitudes and comments of family members can be a stumbling block. More to the point, your own reactions to their attitudes and comments can be a stumbling block.** Two responses on my part hindered me, resentment and fear: resentment that they apparently could see weakness in no one except me, and fear that they would give up on me before I could change enough to suit them. I knew I had made life difficult for their son, but now that I had made a start in recovery, I wanted to be given a fair chance at it.

When I hung up the phone after speaking with John's dad, I wanted to scream, "I'm not the only one with problems here." Incidents like this re-activated my frustrations that no one understood how I felt or how hard I was trying.

The family's part in the sufferer's recovery.

One of the things that irritated me was how my in-laws had related to me in the previous months. During the summer I could tell that they and John were talking about me behind my back. They were guarded around me and held me at arm's length. Something was not right. If they believed my problems were mostly psychological and were earnestly wanting me to see this, why didn't they talk to me about it?

I don't hold this against them now, because I realize they had never been through anything like this either and were feeling their way along, just as I was. Perhaps they feared that I would over-react if they broached the subject (a legitimate concern), or perhaps they did try and I simply don't recall it. In any case, I felt awkward around them for a long time.

If you, the reader, are the family member of a sufferer and you have more insight into the problem than the sufferer does, gently bring up the subject. **Talk *to* the person, not just *about* her. She may be sick, but she's not deaf; she can hear or sense when she's being talked about behind her back. Excluding her is disrespectful if she is capable of being included in the conversation.** Suggest that she see a counselor or doctor. Or show her a list of the symptoms of depression or anxiety and ask if she sees herself in it. Or offer to accompany her to counseling so that she does not feel picked on. For that matter, you probably would benefit from some counseling your-self, because by now you have been through the fire, too.

If you are the sufferer and you do feel that fingers are pointing at you, you might try talking nicely with the accuser(s) about this. But more importantly, face the reality that you cannot change anybody but yourself, and in your present state, you are not going to be very convincing if you try to persuade someone else that he is part of the problem.

John made four or five trips to the hospital so that we could both talk to the social worker. I had such mixed feelings towards him - I felt sorry for him, appreciated him, and was furious with him all at the same time. I could see sadness, fatigue, anger, and fear in his face. He seemed so vulnerable. When I looked at John, I felt affection and pity, but I was torn between wanting to console him and wanting to punch his lights out. It was hard for me to offer him sympathy when I felt that he was unsympathetic towards me.

In one appointment, I became so enraged with John's blaming and lack of empathy that I threw a cup of water in his face (I had one in my hand already because of my dry mouth). I immediately recognized that I had insulted him terribly and should apologize on the spot or we were finished for sure, so I apologized. By venting my exasperation in such an inappropriate way, I had made myself look even worse. John didn't see an extremely miserable person in dire need of emotional support from him. I think all he saw was an immature, heartless person throwing a fit at his expense. I had sabotaged my own cry for help.

On John's first visit to the hospital, he brought Joseph, and my mother babysat. She remembers that John looked like "death warmed over." He may have been in his own depression in reaction to mine. **(It is not unusual for me to discover in my counseling practice that the spouse and/or the children of my**

depressed clients are in their own pits. Frequently they need their own appointments.)

The staff did express to me that John should be visiting more often. When I explained that he had a church and our boys to tend to, plus a three-hour drive, they said that was no excuse because my therapy was important, and he needed to be present to participate with me. I guess they did see our marital issues as significant after all, and they wanted us to work on them jointly.

Get the chip off (your shoulder) and the lead out.

How did I get past the disturbing phone call and the issues it stirred up? By recognizing that I could not do anything to directly change other family members – maybe not ever; but if there was any hope for changing anyone else in the family, I was going to have to begin with myself. I remember stomping out of the room and saying to myself, "Maybe if I get well enough, they will finally take me seriously. For now, I've got a job to do, and I'm going to do it, even if nobody but me ever changes." I couldn't know if my progress would satisfy them or not, but I couldn't afford to dwell on that. I can't say I was feeling magnanimous; I fumed the rest of the night.

A crucial lesson.

You will notice a major theme throughout this book. It's a lesson I learned the hard way and kept having to relearn in one area after another. The point is this: **you are personally accountable to God for your own life, and you are responsible for your own recovery, with God's help, no matter what! In spite of your feeling misunderstood, unappreciated, and discredited. In spite of slow-acting medication and side-effects. In spite of the guilt you feel or others seem to want you to feel. In spite of finger-pointing relatives. NO MATTER WHAT !**

72

Chapter 10

Whose Fault Is This?

For the first half of my stay at St. Mark's, I spent most of my free time alone. I went to the gift shop and browsed; shopping encouraged feelings of normalcy. I bought cards to send to the boys. I walked outdoors in the garden on pretty days and shook my head at my inability to enjoy the flowers and the sunshine. I could appreciate them in a way, but they didn't lift my spirits as they once would have.

I spent time in my room praying, reflecting, and reading my Bible. I was searching for answers and entertaining deeper thoughts than in my ruminations of the previous summer.

Who's to blame?

I considered the matter of who or what was responsible for my depression. For once, I actually did something right; I did not spin my wheels trying to determine blame. The concept of "fault" is not very useful with depression and anxiety. Attempts to determine blame can divert your attention from more constructive endeavors. Even if you could trace your depression to unhealthy parenting or an abusive spouse, does that make the depression the parent's or spouse's fault? I don't think so, but the question is virtually irrelevant.

Some individuals get hung up trying to assess blame and make sure it does not fall on them. Adam blamed Eve, Eve blamed the serpent, and God was not pleased. I have seen clients dig their heels in and refuse to accept responsibility for recovery because they believed that to do so was the equivalent of saying, "I am to blame." Even if the person was "to blame," so what? We all

73

make mistakes, and God will forgive our sins if we sincerely repent. God clearly prefers repentance to misplaced blame.

I did examine possible causes of my depression, hoping to gain some of the insight into myself that the MMPI suggested was lacking. **I have learned since then that depression can be caused by a number of things: loss, chronic stress or abuse, faulty thinking and beliefs, a sense of powerlessness or learned helplessness, unresolved emotional baggage, repressed anger, physical illness or childbirth, chemical imbalances, certain medications, or (according to psychologist Aaron Beck) even a deficit of activities that provide pleasure or a sense of self-efficacy.** I did not have the benefit of such a list when I was trying to understand the factors in my depression, but I figured out a few things anyway.

At the time, what I could see was that I was burned out; responsibilities, illness, and attempts to help solve problems in my own extended family had taken a toll. I do wonder now if a postpartum depression precipitated the whole thing. Genetics, too, were at work in my nervous system, with Daddy, Sarah, and David having also experienced depression and/or panic attacks. And my history suggests an overly-sensitive temperament and a thought life full of extremes and negatives.

I considered whether Satan and evil played a part in my illness. I believed then, and still believe, that Satan and his legions actively stir up doubt, division, and distress. I knew that Satan was probably dancing with glee over me, but, having acknowledged that, I could not see how focusing on him would be constructive.

What about sin?

I gained a new understanding of sin. I could already see sin both as separation from God (and the propensity towards disobedience that this represents) and also as specific acts of that disobedience. Both are Biblical concepts. But now, as I sat on my hospital bed (with the rails down), I could see something more. I began to understand sin more as a condition.

"So this is what we are capable of all by ourselves. This is what we can degenerate into," I thought. I could see that sin involves our twistedness, even our twisted thinking and emotions, and especially our finiteness; there was obviously much that was beyond my understanding or control. **I could see my predicament as part of a fallen world – with fallen minds, fallen moods, fallen relationships, fallen bodies -** and as the result of these things not only in my own life, but in the life of preceding generations, our extended families, and our culture. **I had wanted to be seen as part of the human race. Now I could see that I was part of humanity in all its frailty.** The word "wretch" in the song "Amazing Grace" seemed powerfully accurate to me.

I truly did not get this way in a vacuum. This world I lived in extended way beyond my little nest. I began to see myself and others more from God's perspective. I was one member of a whole race of sinful, limited, selfish people. The death and decay brought on by Original Sin was apparent, and it was being played out in me.

Then what about blame? To the extent that we are all sinners in need of grace, we are all to blame. The idea that sin had contributed to my depression made sense now. It was a helpful idea, not a threatening one. What was the downward spiral of my disorders if not evidence of a fallen world? Did this mean that I was faithless or that God had abandoned me? No. It did mean that **I was dependent on the grace of God. If things could be this bad with God in the picture, what would happen to us if He were to withdraw His hand from the planet?** "There but for the grace of God go I." And you.

This may sound depressing, but for me it was liberating. I wondered why I hadn't caught on sooner. **This understanding allowed me to see myself, and every other person I knew, in a new light. I could see in each life both the causes and the results of sin. I could forgive myself and others.**

Albert Ellis, the founder of Rational-Emotive Behavior Therapy (originally just Rational-Emotive Therapy), is not of the Christian faith, but he makes a point that is consistent with what we believe as Christians. He has noted the tendency of every individual to do that which is irrational or, as he puts it, self-defeating. He is right, though I would go one step further and say that we not only have a bent towards hurting and sabotaging ourselves; we also tend towards hurting God and rebelling or working against Him.

To choose not to grow is to choose to regress.

What does this sin stuff mean? It means that if we don't depend on God, any of us is capable of winding up somewhere we wouldn't want to be.

It also means that living in a victorious, healthy, mature way requires effort and intentionality. To do nothing is to let nature take its course.

Jesus's parables are full of the imagery of planting, tending, and harvesting, so that a desirable crop would be produced. Somebody was WORKING in these parables. Farmers nurtured their fields, vineyard owners their vines, parents their children, and God us.

God expects our participation in our own growth. You cannot expect the fruit of the Holy Spirit in your life if you do not abide in Christ. "Abide" means to "rest" or "dwell," activities which don't really sound all that active. However, in John 15:10,

Jesus says that we will abide in his love if we keep his commandments. Obedience requires action; Jesus spent a great deal of time telling us what to do, not just what not to do. We are to take up our cross daily, digest God's Word, and consciously, intentionally love God and people. Discipline, sacrifice, time, sweat, and fresh starts may be involved in recovery and growth. Is it worth it? The fruit of the Holy Spirit includes joy and peace, so the answer for me was "yes."

We talk about the symptoms of depression, but **depression itself is a symptom. As with physical pain, it is a signal that something is wrong and needs to be fixed.** It may be that the nervous system needs chemical help to run more efficiently. Your lifestyle may need adjusting; or your relationship to God or others; or your thoughts and beliefs. In my case, the latter needed a major over-haul, not just a tune-up; I will go into this in a later chapter.

Try to look at your emotional disturbances as an OPPORTUNITY rather than a burden. This is your chance to become more the person that you have probably said you want to be. In fact, this is your chance to become more Christlike.

<u>**Accepting responsibility for recovery is more important than figuring out how you got sick.**</u>

Perhaps God will show you the causes of your problems now, perhaps later, and possibly not at all. But rest assured: **whether or not you determine each and every factor that contributed to your illness, you can still recover and grow. Healthy living is healthy living, and you can learn to do, say, and think more of the right things without knowing precisely how you came to be unhealthy.** Down the line, after you see which changes have made the most difference for you, you may finally determine the original sources of your problems.

After my release from St. Mark's, I joined a twelve-step "mutual support" group called GROW, Inc. One of their best principles concerns responsibility, and it would be appropriate to share here. It comes from their little blue book:

> **However I came to be sick, it is my responsibility to get well.** Sick behaviour [sic] and wrong behaviour are the same disorderly behaviour viewed from the angle of who is most to blame. But it is certainly wrong to blame others entirely for my present disorders and difficulties, wrong to hark back to past causes to excuse present inactivity and unwillingness to change, wrong to stay sick when I can learn to get well, and wrong not to accept necessary help.

> **Sickness, by making it harder for me, makes it my duty to try harder.** I still have to do what is right and avoid what is wrong in my present circumstances.

In central Illinois, one popular site is Rockome Gardens. In the midst of each flower garden is a sign with a saying written on it. A colorful photo which I took of one of these signs and its surroundings hangs in my office. It reads: **"None of us is responsible for all the things that happen to us, but all of us are responsible for the way we act when they do happen."**

Focusing on my own recovery in St. Mark's was a full-time job. Placing blame and searching for causes at great length would have been a waste of time.

Chapter 11

What About Me?

It was time to deal with Self. I had a lot of work to do here.

My first week I did not particularly want to mix with the other patients. Once at mealtime I took my tray to my room and began eating off the bedtable. The nurse came in and insisted that I join the others. She did not accept my explanation for why I wanted to eat alone, so I begrudgingly joined the others. Later I socialized more and even enjoyed it, but not at this point.

Exception to the rule?

I share this incident because it represented something about my thinking that may also be true of your thinking. Individuals who are depressed or anxious, especially if they are also lacking in self-confidence and somewhat passive, may see themselves as exceptions to the rule. It's part of the "But you don't understand" mentality. I had no problem with there being rules; I just wanted to be excused from following them.

I was not this way across the board, but I can see that, even in everyday living, I had a different set of expectations for myself than for everybody else. Sometimes, I expected a great deal of myself when I would have let others off the hook. Other times, because I feared failure or humiliation, I withdrew from what everyone else was doing and demanded very little of myself. The nurse, without explaining her rationale, wanted me to **drop any expectations for special treatment and toughen up**.

Lose the self-pity.

My self-concept was distorted in more ways than one. I did expect allowances to be made. None were, not even for the weakness I still felt from the pneumonia. And I'm sure you can see that I was reeking of self-pity, though I would not have called it that. I felt like a victim, a martyr, and I wanted comfort and encouragement. Did I want people to feel sorry for me? Probably.

Pastor and counselor Tim LaHaye, author of *How to Win Over Depression*, maintains that self-pity is at the heart of all depressions. An attitude of self-pity does seem prominent. **Even if the person is not self-pitying in the beginning, indulging in "poor me" thoughts can become a nasty habit after she has felt bad for a while.** In my case, I think the self-pity was both a cause of and one result of my disorders. I definitely needed to get over it.

Finding a healthy appreciation of self.

Another problem that I had was with self-esteem. I heard myself described by Dan Allender, author of *The Wounded Heart*, at a workshop in 1994. He explained that it is **possible to simultaneously have both too high and too low an opinion of yourself.** I had begun to see this while in St. Mark's. I was associating with people whom I was inclined to look down on, yet sometimes I didn't join them for fear of feeling inadequate. What a contradiction!

I began to see myself and others as equals. Occasionally in group, a person towards whom I might once have turned up my nose would share the most profound wisdom. This was humbling in a good way. **I discovered that every person has something**

80

to contribute to or share with others. I gained a new openness and respect for all kinds of people.

I began to look for new foundations for feeling good about myself. It was clear that if my value as a person was based on my intellectual prowess, my musical ability, my appearance, or my standing with other people, I was clearly not worth much at this time. This seemed neither good nor accurate.

For example, I had once played five three-part classical pieces on the piano, by memory, before a "judge." Now, when I would sit down at the piano in our exercise room, my fingers were so tight and shaky that I could not play "Row, Row, Row Your Boat"; in fact, simply reading the music was hard because my hand-eye coordination was so poor. I clearly couldn't base my self-worth on musical accomplishments.

And what of family? The awareness that John might not take me back undermined my self-esteem.

I found myself wondering, "If I am valuable, what makes me so? Why do I count at all, if I do?" **Before leaving St. Mark's, I would find a Biblical foundation for my self-worth, but for a little while there was a vacuum in this area.**

Many of the lessons I was learning in St. Mark's were confirmed for me later in GROW. For instance, GROW's Principle of Ordinariness is helpful if you tend to have an opinion of yourself that is too high and/or too low or based on performance. It goes like this: **"I can be ordinary. I can do whatever ordinary good people do, and avoid whatever ordinary good people avoid. My special abilities will develop in harmony only if my foremost aim is to be a good ordinary human being."** We do not have to be outstanding or perfect. I caught glimpses of this as I sat in group, warmed by the presence of other individuals who were also simply trying to be healthy, decent human beings and to help each other.

Decentralize. Seek a more balanced view.

I knew I needed to get myself out of the center of the picture. GROW's Principle of Decentralization expresses this well: **"Decentralize situations and events from yourself and look for the total view, which includes others as equals in a God-centered and growth-oriented perspective."** That is, the world doesn't revolve around any one of us - just me or just you. Other people count, and God oversees the whole big picture, which includes all of us in balanced perspective.

I should not over-react or distort something just because it involves or affects me. I would also add that the measure of something's importance does not lie exclusively in how it relates to me. A piece of furniture or an idea or an activity is no less valuable to others just because I don't appreciate it. And my belongings, needs, and thoughts are not more important than somebody else's.

I had never seen nor heard of GROW at that time, but the lessons I was learning in St. Mark's were confirmed for me later when I would read a GROW statement and rejoice, "Yes! That's it!" Confirmation that I was on the right track was uplifting, and the "right track" began being laid for me in the hospital.

My own self-absorption began evolving into a healthy self-awareness at St. Mark's as I gradually dropped the whining and worrying and also began to balance the introspection with some attention to other people. I had been living in my own little reality, and it was time to stick my head out of the shell again and rejoin the rest of the world.

I have found an assignment that I did on this subject. I wrote: "I know myself better than anybody, and **I should be willing to take time for myself. Also, to stick up for myself. However, my real satisfaction and meaning in life come through my relationships with other people. I need to get my mind off myself.**"

Jesus tells us in Mark 12:31 to "love your neighbor AS yourself," not "Love your neighbor instead of yourself" or "yourself instead of your neighbor." We are to love others neither more nor less than we love ourselves.

I began to learn about co-dependency. I needed to improve in the areas of real self-care (not babying myself); to not depend on John so much; and to relate to people in ways other than rescuing, controlling, fixing, appeasing, or "enabling" their doing these things. In other words, I needed to stop expecting other people to do those things that fell in the realm of my responsibility. And I needed to stop worrying about the stuff that falls within other people's boundaries. This world of adults in CTU provided an arena in which I could initiate some of these changes in myself.

Are you out of balance in your focus, or in your giving and receiving? If you feel empty because you have given so much to others, take a little time for yourself. If, however, you have been preoccupied with yourself, make a point to do something for someone else. You might even find somebody who is worse off than you are. Our communities abound with lonely, incapacitated, and grieving individuals. Visit someone, or make a phone call, or send a card. Do not wait until you feel fine. Focusing on someone else's needs instead of your own could be therapeutic for both of you.

This is love?

I began to understand more about mature love, which is a

83

healthy balance between soft love and tough love. This concept was not totally new to me, because I had offered both to my children, and I believe I did so appropriately all my parenting years except for parts of 1984.

However, relating to adults was a different story. I had difficulty with tough love, which is the part of caring that involves accountability, discipline, and sometimes confrontation. I never expressed to other adults anything that they might not want to hear, because I didn't want to hurt their feelings, and I wanted to be liked. I was a people-pleaser. Also, when someone was critical of me, I experienced a sense of inadequacy and rejection. When John expressed some anger towards me in a joint session at St. Mark's, I had a hard time handling it, even though this exercise was supposed to be therapeutic for both of us. Tough love was being shown to me in CTU, and I had to adjust to the idea that this was "love" at all.

I could exchange soft love - gentleness, compassion, encouragement, and affection - with adults, though I hadn't done much of this lately. I needed to resume these efforts, though I wanted to go one step farther and be certain that the soft love I offered was for the right reasons. Was I being good to people because I cared about them and they would benefit, or did I just need to feel needed? Did giving to people allow me to feel superior? Was it a way of avoiding facing my own issues? Or did I genuinely care? Having accepted responsibility for change, I questioned some things for the first time.

I hope that I am offering you both kinds of love in this book. The encouragement and understanding are the soft part; the challenges are the tough part.

Why is this talk of love relevant to recovery? Because you can't be mentally and emotionally healthy if your attitudes and relationships are unhealthy, and vice versa. I definitely moved more consistently towards recovery when I could accept the accountability and responsibility of tough love. Check yourself for your ability to receive tough love; give tough love; receive soft love; and give soft love. All of these are important if you're going to experience the joy and peace of the Christian life.

Signs of progress.

About the time I was coming to a new appreciation of the people around me, I read a book suggested in our bibliotherapy group. It piqued my interest, because we had seen a video of the author, Leo Buscaglia, speaking to a crowd, and his style was endearing. The book was a compilation of heart-warming stories by Buscaglia called *Living, Loving, and Learning*. **I was reminded of the healing power of love, laughter and hugs**. I almost enjoyed reading the book. I remember smiling to myself and thinking, "Some aspects of getting well might not be so hard and might even be fun." Buscaglia reminded me how good life can be, especially the simple things.

A couple of contrasting incidents demonstrate that I was progressing in the eyes of the staff. The second week of my stay, I attempted to mediate between two people in one of our groups. This sounds admirable, but the counselor told me that I should not be doing this until I had accomplished more in my own recovery. She said my attempt represented avoidance of my own issues. Three weeks later, I extended a helping hand to someone, and the counselor congratulated me. In fact, she chided the others for not doing the same. Why did she see my reaching out as a good thing at that point? Because it was in better balance with proper attention to my own problems. I was learning more about how to love both myself and others.

By the way, when I had attempted to mediate, the counselor's discouragement did not mean that I had nothing to offer. My intuition and conciliatory skills turned out to be real, and I use them now in doing marriage and family counseling. **Do not let your current situation cause you to question whether you have anything to offer the world. God will use you and your gifts when the time is right.** That could be today, or it could be much later.

Chapter 12

"You Should Be Grateful!"

Where were the other people in my life? Daddy called me frequently from his home in Houston to see how I was doing. Rosemary, my lifelong friend, called more than once. Talking to her was a normalizing experience. John's parents visited me once on a Sunday afternoon. Our visit went much more smoothly than the phone call had, and I appreciated their making the trip. I don't think the telephone conversation was mentioned.

A number of friends, including other pastor's wives, sent get-well cards and letters, which I saved with a rubber band around them. I have just now pulled them out of storage, and I counted sixty of them. These meant a lot to me - I had not gotten lost or been forgotten. Friends from our church wrote that they missed me and were praying for me. Nobody mentioned the kind of illness I had, except that one woman wrote about her own experience with "nerves."

Rosemary and my Aunt Mildred each wrote to me several times. Rosemary sent me a "Guideposts" magazine and an advent calendar. Aunt Mildred sent me a goodie box and some cash to spend in the gift shop. I saved it until I could actually enjoy spending it. I received cards with individual signatures from the women's group at church and from Cub Scout Den 3, Nathan's den. If anyone felt awkward about writing to a mental patient, it didn't show.

Nobody else came to visit, but I didn't expect this with the distances involved. A lot of the people in our church helped out at the house with meals, babysitting, and yardwork. Also, John's parents helped him out for a few days, as did Sarah (my sister). I was pleased that he was getting some relief.

People mean well, but....

I toyed with the idea of how people could have been more helpful to me personally, in case I ever found myself in their place. Mostly what I came up with were things they could have avoided saying. I did not receive as many disparaging remarks from acquaintances and friends as some patients did, but I heard my share: things like "Can't you just snap out of it?" and "Just turn it over to the Lord" and "Are you sure there aren't some sins that you haven't confessed?" The most hurtful were "Just pray about it" and "Have you prayed about this?" as if I hadn't thought of that. Most depressed Christians are already praying. And the words "just pray" suggest that if you do this earnestly enough and often enough, no other help will be needed. Though I do know of instances where prayer and waiting were enough, I know of more situations where God also asked the person to do something.

How do you deal with the harsh things that are said to you when you are already down? Forgive. The speaker probably means well and truly does not know how heavy such words fall. Perhaps he or she is uninformed about depression and anxiety. And do the obvious, which is to **make sure that you have not let anything come between you and the Lord, because, now and then, those harsh words contain a little truth.**

Prayer - difficult but important.

I want to add here that if you do have trouble praying, you are not alone. The odds are that you did pray for quite a while, and then you felt too bad to pray, or you have given up because praying seemed to make no difference. The detached or distanced feeling that accompanies depression can cause you to feel that God is not hearing you and possibly is not even there at all. If there have been times in your life when you did *feel* God's presence, it is especially disconcerting to not experience this now.

God has not moved; He is still listening, so pray if you can. Simple prayers are fine. Praying is just conversing with God, and this does not need to sound profound or pretty. Be honest. Just try to keep the communication lines open. **And ask other people to pray for you.** I had only one short stretch where I did not pray as much, and it meant a lot to me to know that others were praying through that time.

The prayers of friends can be very powerful, as when the men lowered their friend through the roof so that Jesus could heal him (Lk. 5). Intercessory prayers carry or lift the person before Jesus. My sister had learned this through the hard times in her own life. Sarah also understood better than most the heaviness of my depression, so she was especially committed to prayer during this time.

I still have a letter in which Sarah wrote, "I have pledged myself to be the best prayer warrior the Lord will allow me to be," and she promised to pray for me and for John on a regular basis and every time the Lord nudged her. I have no doubts that she did precisely this. She added this humorous touch, "If I called you every time the Lord nudged me to pray for you in order to confirm the reason, we'd have no food or furnishings because the phone bills would be so high." I know I never properly thanked Sarah or the many other individuals who prayed for me. I really appreciated them.

Gratitude – what it will and will not do.

One day someone reminded me of my family and home and said, "You have so much to be grateful for. What are you doing here?" Statements like this heaped on the condemnation. I knew I had much to be grateful for and the implications that I was not grateful and that gratitude alone should pull me out of the pit were insulting.

89

If someone has made this kind of remark to you, remember that they are simply trying to be helpful, and that they may feel at a loss, too. Sometimes individuals don't know what else to say. They are not meaning to insult you. In your overly-sensitive state, you may take things too negatively and too personally. And, as I said earlier, forgive. Even if the "consoler" does seem mean-spirited, harboring resentment over his or her remarks will only hinder *your* progress.

While on the topic of gratitude, let me say this: **I have heard it said that the characteristic most closely associated with good mental health is an attitude of gratitude. I accept this, but I believe that once a person is seriously depressed, more is required for recovery than cultivating the practice of thanksgiving.**

Having said that, let me emphasize that focusing on the positive and then giving God the credit are vital; don't expect to get well if you are NOT doing this. First of all, gratitude naturally combats self-pity. It is virtually impossible to be focusing on your blessings and feeling sorry for yourself at the same time. Secondly, to thank God is to honor Him as the giver of all good things, including life and restoration, and I believe He honors us in return.

Even though I knew I had much to be grateful for, I did not FEEL grateful for a while, because this feeling was squashed along with other good ones. At that time I did make a vow which, for the most part, I have kept. **Because I was missing the ability to feel good things – pleasure, interest, thankfulness – I promised God that if I ever recovered my ability to feel these things, I would not take these feelings for granted. Also, I would not take the blessings themselves for granted.** I would "enjoy" all the big and little pleasures in life (within moral and reasonable limits). When good feelings began to return to me after a few more days, I was very grateful!

Chapter 13

He'll Think I'm Crazy!

I probably could have secured more information and support if I had opened up more and asked more questions, but I was confused as to what it was and wasn't okay to talk about. I did not tell the doctor about my panic attacks nor ask anyone what causes them. I really thought I would hear "You've gotta be crazy!" if I did share my concerns, symptoms and weird sensations. **They sounded bizarre even to me, so how could others not think they were bizarre?** At least, that's what I thought. Also, I could have asked for the rationale behind some of what we were doing in our program, but I didn't. I didn't want to risk being degraded or scolded. I wish I had asked.

If you are getting treatment, don't be afraid to ask questions or express your concerns. Nothing you can say will surprise the experienced professional. Also, he or she will probably be willing to discuss your concerns so long as you listen and don't just spout off. The therapist does not want to be discounted any more than you do, or to waste his or her breath.

Ask for the professional's rationale, if knowing this will increase your confidence in his or her recommendations. However, trusting others may be part of what you have to learn here, so don't be too disgruntled if the therapist or doctor doesn't explain everything.

It will always be tough to know how much to educate yourself on your medications and how much to simply trust the doctor. Things actually can go wrong, but trust that your doctor doesn't want this any more than you do. Some things you may be better off not knowing, if you are a worrier.

My withholding some from the staff may have compromised their ability to help me, but on the other hand, it encouraged me to help myself. My sense that I was largely on my own fueled a healthy resourcefulness and the sense that I was responsible for my own progress. Most of my new insights dawned while I was alone with God in my room. Sure, I would have benefited from more personal guidance, but **I was in a balancing act regarding how much I should look to others for help. While I wish I had discussed things more freely with the staff, I do not regret one moment that I spent alone praying, planning, and reflecting.**

Relaxation techniques.

One area in which I learned to reach out was in practicing **relaxation techniques**. Let me explain these. The theory behind these is that **the emotional tension a person experiences manifests itself in the muscles, and this muscle tension then further exacerbates the emotional tension. Learning to relax the muscles can lead to a deeper sense of peace throughout the body.** We were led through two different kinds of exercises, and I definitely had a preference.

I had some trouble with **Progressive Muscle Relaxation**, though I have since learned to use it. The reason it was difficult for me is that it requires you to focus on the sensations in different parts of your body, while tensing and then relaxing various muscle groups in succession. The rationale is sound, but at the time, physical sensations were a source of anxiety for me, and when I became too conscious of them, panic ensued. I've heard of other individuals experiencing this same relaxation-induced anxiety, though more people find PMR beneficial than detrimental.

The technique which was effective for me required **visualization**. The therapist took us on guided imagery trips to the woods or the beach. Thoughts of peaceful places can calm jangled nerves, and I found that I could actually "let go." The feeling of floating or falling was strange at first, but my being able to do it meant I was capable of feeling less bound up; it also meant that I was trusting the therapist to a healthy degree.

I did not "tune out" or give up my will, and there was nothing inappropriate in these exercises - no "inner guide" (a New Age proposition which can put you in touch with demonic forces), and no emptying of the mind. **I am not using or recommending anything that would cause you to lose control of yourself or your consciousness. Do not seek to become a passive receptacle of whatever may come to you. Instead actively focus on something that is positive. The imagination is God's gift and is a blessing when used under His control. I find the relaxation imagery consistent with Paul's suggestion in the fourth chapter of Philippians that we think about good things.** Nature is God's handiwork, so reflecting on it seems appropriate. You can use the 23rd Psalm and imagine yourself with the Good Shepherd if this appeals to you.

I wrote the following after one of my early experiences with visualization. We were to picture ourselves in a hot-air balloon:

> As I relaxed I felt as if I were light and my body was
> falling. I felt very relaxed, but as if I were losing control
> [only a sensation--it occurs when your muscles are
> relaxing for the first time in a long time]. My balloon
> floated very high over the snow-covered mountains
> of Austria and Switzerland. In the valleys and lowlands
> I could see little white churches and villages, like the
> ones we saw on our trip to Europe. The green was so
> green, and the white was so white. John and I were
> both in the balloon. I don't know if the boys were
> with us. I think they were, and I was pointing things
> out to them.

I began to like the free feeling and once or twice actually sought out someone to help me do the exercises. She could have turned me down, a risk I was willing to take, but she didn't. I eventually was able to lie on my own bed, reproducing the imagery and varying it as I chose, and capturing the same sense of peace by myself. Meanwhile, my reaching out meant that I was learning to trust someone besides myself in this recovery process - a good sign.

Before my admission to St. Mark's I had done a lot of leaning on John. I am not sure that I trusted him, yet I expected him to somehow fix my problems or make everything all right. I had not seen myself as a mature woman, capable of doing the things other people do. This view was not reasonable, but it partially explains why I expected special treatment and why I thought someone else should make things easy for me - if not John, then a doctor or someone else. My tendency to look to someone else to rescue me did not go away overnight.

So how was my seeking out the therapist a GOOD thing? Because the kind of leaning I was beginning to do now was not so much leaning as it was learning. I could look to someone who could show me how to help myself instead of whining and expecting them to fix things for me. Also, I was getting myself out of the double bind of depending on people without actually trusting them, a predicament which might have kept me stuck. I was also being able to, at least occasionally, discern more specifically what my problem was (muscle tension), to say so, and to be willing to try a corresponding solution.

[If you are interested in learning how to do relaxation exercises, check out *The Anxiety & Phobia Workbook* by Edmund J. Bourne or *The Relaxation & Stress Reduction Workbook* by Martha Davis, Elizabeth Robbins Eshelman, and Matthew McKay.]

Chapter 14

Can't You Speed Things Up?

The CTU program had several components to it: classes in self-awareness and assertiveness training; group therapy; weekly meetings; expressive therapy (art and music modes); and bibliotherapy (reading and discussing specific books with the group). Ceramics and exercise were optional, and I did not participate; the MMPI interpreter had been right about me – I wanted no part of anything that might create more anxiety, even if it might be fun, and for some reason I feared failure or making a fool of myself in these activities.

Appointments with Dr. Mason and Jenny, our social worker, were expected. I saw Dr. Mason daily for fifteen or twenty minutes, and Jenny every few days for an hour or so. When John came up, we met with Jenny. More than once I talked with Drew, one of the chaplains.

Angry?

On one occasion, Drew suggested that perhaps I had a lot of pent-up anger from the past and I should express it using the empty-chair technique. He set an empty chair opposite me, and I was to imagine that the person I was angry with was sitting there and then express my anger to that person any way I wanted. At that time I wasn't conscious of feeling angry towards anyone except John, but I knew that wasn't what Drew was looking for. He was looking for anger I had repressed, which by definition is anger that the person is not aware of having or feeling. I sat down and tried to think of who I might be angry with.

A few ideas came to mind, but no spontaneous emotion was forthcoming, so I felt no relief. I learned something from this exercise: **timing is important**. Trying to pull memories out of a hat on demand did not work. Repressed feelings, if there are any, have been repressed because facing and feeling them would be difficult. The barrier that has kept them repressed doesn't vanish immediately just because someone else wants it to. I attempted to comply with Drew, but I felt manipulated. Old memories and the accompanying emotions can be accessed, but I have since found that this will happen more naturally if the person is ready, i.e., if she has moved to this point at her own pace and has a safe setting and relationship in which to let go. I'd had very little time with Drew, and on a whim he wanted me to dig deep; without security or transition, I couldn't respond to a chair plopped in front of me.

For some people, unexpressed anger is one of the causes of their depression (and their short fuse). If you are one of those people, then you do need to vent that anger when you are ready. If you really need to let go in an uninhibited way, you can use the empty-chair technique or write a letter you never send. If it's possible and safe for you, and you can control yourself, you can confront the person directly, if this seems advisable. Do not vent indiscriminately, because doing so perpetuates cycles of hurt, anger, or abuse.

Feeling good, if only for a moment...

A week or so into my stay, my mother left to return to Arkansas. She could see that I had settled into a routine and was not going to be discharged anytime soon. I was busy enough that her departure did not leave a gaping hole.

The rules in CTU allowed us to leave the open unit and move around the building and grounds, so long as we checked in every couple of hours. We could leave the grounds if we had a pass from the doctor, but I had no way to take advantage of this opportunity without a car. Some patients had their own vehicles in the hospital parking lot, and they came and went more freely.

96

One night Ann, my roommate Dana, and I signed out of the unit together and undertook an excursion around the hospital interior. We were not permitted to venture into every part but we could explore a few floors. All three of us had taken Xanax, and we were feeling GOOOOD! We traipsed around feeling giddy and free. We laughed a lot, probably loudly, and had a marvelous time. This was the first time in an eternity that I had laughed, and I was enjoying it, even if medication did get the credit.

At one point Dana, whose car was outside, suggested that perhaps we should go out for an evening on the town. We did not have passes and did not follow through, but the very idea gave us something to chatter about. I was in stitches thinking what we would look like.

Memories of a scene from the movie *Nine to Five* came to me - the scene where the three hysterical women are driving crazily and then get pulled over by a police officer. I had visions of the three of us being stopped and an officer looking at our hospital bracelets. With our giddy antics, we would have looked exactly like the mental patients we were.

But the hits just keep on comin'.

At this time, smoking was allowed in designated areas of the hospital, and the smoke wafted its way all over our unit. Everybody - patients and staff alike - smoked, with only one or two exceptions. I was one of those exceptions, and I have an allergy to smoke. My mouth and throat, already dry from the Elavil, were burning from this exposure. My hay fever flared up, and an internist was called in to treat my latest problem. Also, acne had spread across my back and chest, I supposed as another side effect from the medicine. I don't remember what the internist did for either of these developments, but I remember wondering when I would have fewer ailments instead of more.

One night an incident occurred which challenged my ability to handle more anxiety. Dana had a heart condition, about which I never learned any details. Apparently it could be serious when it flared, and one night it flared. We had just gone to bed, and I was not asleep. Without saying anything to me, she beeped for the nurses. After one arrived and checked on her, some kind of alarm went out over the sound system for other medical personnel to come to our room. While a group of people surrounded Dana doing who knows what, I lay quietly on my bed, trying not to panic.

I cannot explain why Dana's emergency frightened me so much, but it did. I guess the implicit thought was, "If this could happen to her, could it also happen to me?" Or perhaps I feared having to be responsible for her sometime. I didn't ask anyone what was going on, because they were too busy to answer me, but I was terribly relieved when the crisis had passed.

I began to mingle more with the other patients. In the evening we played card games and Scrabble in the dining room, while songs from the radio were piped over the sound system. I discovered that I could whip the socks off of everybody in Scrabble, an encouraging experience for me. At least my mind had not totally gone to pot.

A less encouraging moment of enlightenment occurred in group. We had been given one of those exercises such as you find in *Values Clarification* by Simon, Howe, and Kirschenbaum. I don't remember if we were supposed to be on a desert island or escaping a sinking vessel or building something together. A certain number of roles were delineated, and we had to select which person in the group would be best suited for each role. Nobody chose me for anything (there were more roles than people). I realized that I still had a lot of ground to cover if even this group could not spot any noteworthy strengths in me.

Time dragged, and so did signs of recovery. **I wanted to be better NOW, not tomorrow, not next week, not next month.** I could identify with the Proverb "Hope deferred makes the heart sick" (13:12a). The days were coming and going, mostly gray and chilly. More than once it snowed, and I looked out at a sight that normally would have thrilled me. Would we have a white Christmas? Would I be home in time? Would I even be capable of enjoying Christmas?

In spite of the fact that I was learning about helpful techniques, such as how to relax my muscles, I kept looking for the one magic remedy, the key that would explain or fix virtually anything. I wanted something simple, swift and obvious – and preferably handed to me by somebody else.

A victory.

While I was waiting for signs of progress and for some mystical light to dawn, a wondrous thing happened. A light did dawn.

The incident began like this: a handful of us were watching the movie *The Right Stuff* in the same room where I had "slept" my first night at St. Mark's. It was the first time I had opted to watch anything with the others.

The visual effects in a particular scene sent me into a tailspin. The test pilot, Chuck Yeager, was pushing his aircraft to fly faster than anyone had ever flown before, and we, the audience, were to sense that we were seeing things from his point of view. The movie-maker's intent was accomplished with me: confined in this small, dark room, with nothing to see but speeding, spinning images on the screen, and no reference point for distinguishing up from down, I felt as disoriented and out-of-control as the pilot who lost control of the plane. The worst panic attack of my life overtook me in a split second.

I left the room and walked briskly back to the open unit. As I went I thought about asking the nurses for a Xanax. After all, I could have one as needed, and I was in desperate need. As I approached room 558, I realized that asking for a pill was pointless. By now I knew that most of my attacks only lasted for a few minutes (though it seemed like hours); by the time the Xanax would be in my system, the attack would be over. The pill would not meet my need for immediate relief.

I sat on the end of Dana's bed, which was nearer to the door than mine, restraining myself from bolting down the hall or asking for help. I thought, "One of two things will happen. Either this will kill me (in which case nothing would have saved me in time) or it will pass." I resolved to hang on for the ride. I don't know how much time passed, but the symptoms finally began to subside.

I pondered what had happened. I had just beaten, or at least survived, the most intense terror and the most disconcerting sensations. I still wanted someone to hand me a cure. I did not want to be fully responsible for fixing myself, because I wasn't sure I could do it. However, I could see for the first time that if I allowed my "cure" to lie in the hands of something or somebody else, then someone else would always have the power to steal my health or peace or to withhold them from me. If I could find within myself the ability to cope, then I would be self-contained, so to speak. Nobody could give me peace, but perhaps nobody would be able to take it away, either! I felt a spark of hope and resolved to become stronger.

I have never had another panic attack of this intensity. The knowledge that I had survived this one gave me confidence and reassured me that even the worst ones will eventually pass. I did not dread the panic attacks as much after this.

Many keys, but no magic.

It was time to stop the waiting game. Though I had not meant to hold myself back, I had inadvertently done so by expecting something different from what I was getting. Everything I needed was right here, and I had been looking for something more or something different, something easier or more profound or more crystallized.

I wrote the following as part of my homework one day: "Right now is the time for me to get my life figured out. There are people here who are willing to help me. I should trust them more. If I want to function as a healthy person with my family, I must make progress now. I shouldn't keep looking somewhere else or waiting for the perfect person and time to help me out. The people are available at this point in time."

I needed to trust that the program and the people were giving me what I needed, but NOT expect them to make it work for me. Then I needed to use every resource from without and within to assume control over my own life. I was sorting out what I could and could not expect from others. This was my life; if I wasn't going to live it, who was? I was also catching on that "THE solution" was probably more accurately "the solutions," plural, and that one magic key did not exist.

Several weeks after I had been discharged, John and I rented *The Right Stuff* and watched it, snuggling on our bed. I had no negative reactions to the movie, and in fact had trouble identifying the scene that had triggered my panic. This was something of a test to see how strong I was, and passing it was a real triumph for me.

101

ME to control my anxiety
instead of
my Anxiety
controlling me

When I wish upon a star, I wish for...

(expressive therapy - third week; done in bright colors)

Chapter 15

How Do I Do That?

I was allowed to make an overnight trip home. It was good to be with John and the boys, and I did not want to go back to St. Mark's. However, I managed to conclude the visit with a fit of anger towards John, a scene which ended the trip on a sour note for all of us, because the boys witnessed everything. I was obviously not ready to remain at home.

The Elavil began to do its thing, finally. The first change was in the area of eating. I did not feel any different otherwise, but at least food began to look appetizing; in fact, I looked forward to breakfast and wolfed it down. I had forgotten that food could taste so good. Dr. Mason told me later that Elavil had an appetite stimulant in it.

Snack foods looked good, too. I had been an avid consumer of chocolate and Dr. Pepper before, but in recent weeks they had held no appeal. A bag of chocolate chip cookies which Mama had bought for me had remained in my nightstand drawer untouched. All at once I remembered them. Over a period of days I ate the whole bag and didn't even share.

Stop worrying? How?

In my appointments with Dr. Mason, he mostly monitored how I was doing on the Elavil. He left the other therapy up to Jenny and CTU. I do remember one appointment with him because of how exasperated I became.

He said to me, "You've got to stop worrying so much."

I responded, "If I knew how to do that, I wouldn't be here!" I knew he was right; I just didn't know what to do about it.

I had been reading Bible verses about worry. For example, "Do not let not your heart be troubled and do not be afraid" (Jn. 14:27b), and "Therefore I tell you, do not worry about your life.... Who of you by worrying can add a single hour to his life?.....Therefore do not worry about tomorrow, for tomorrow will worry about itself. Each day has enough trouble of its own" (Mt. 6: 25, 27, 34). I also had read Paul's words in Philippians 4:6: "Do not be anxious about anything." I had been regularly presenting my requests "by prayer and petition with thanksgiving," but still I felt anxious.

These verses were commands, like Dr. Mason's. They were good, but they didn't tell me HOW not to worry, or HOW not to be anxious.

Reprogramming my mind.

Another of my moments of insight occurred immediately after I won a game of Scrabble, as I relished my victory, and the insight propelled me towards some answers to the question of how to stop worrying. I reasoned, **"Apparently some parts of my mind work just fine. I've got to figure out how to draw upon the sound parts and use them to help me re-program the unhealthy parts."** I could conceptualize a battle going on in my brain, and I was determined that the "good" side would win.

[I was thrilled recently to find my own conclusion re-stated by Jeffrey Schwartz of UCLA who works with Obsessive-Compulsive Disorder patients. He was quoted by *Newsweek* (January 26, 1998) as saying that patients can break their destructive mental cycles by "willfully activating healthy circuits to predominate over the unhealthy ones." More eloquent - same idea.]

Shortly after this, my re-programming found its impetus:

1) **I discovered the scripture, "Be transformed by the renewing of your mind... ," a part of Romans 12:2 which I adopted as a principle for what I was undertaking.**

2) **In group I received a handout on twisted thinking which would help with the transformation.** It was based on the work of Aaron Beck, a leading figure in cognitive-behavior theory and therapy.

The group leader gave us an extremely brief explanation of the rationale for the handout. He said that **between every experience and our emotional reaction to it, we have a thought, and it is actually this thought which determines the nature of the emotional reaction that follows.** He gave the example of a person walking into a room in which a group of other people are gathered and talking among themselves. Just as the individual enters the room, the other people laugh. If the person assumes that the laughter was in response to him, he may feel embarrassed or humiliated. If he assumes that the laughter pertains to a topic already under discussion before he entered, he will feel more neutral or even anticipate joining the conversation. This made sense to me. If I could change my thoughts in a given situation, I could change how I felt.

I ran down **the list of cognitive distortions that can lead to emotional distress**, and I recognized myself in all but one. "No wonder I have problems," I thought. Here are a few of the "styles of distorted thinking," taken directly from the handout:

Filtering: You take the negative details and magnify them while filtering out all positive aspects of a situation.
Polarized Thinking: Things are black or white, good or bad. You have to be perfect or you're a failure. There is no middle ground.

Overgeneralization: You come to a general conclusion based on a single incident or piece of evidence. If something bad happens once you expect it to happen over and over again.

Catastrophizing: You expect disaster. You notice or hear about a problem and start "What if's:" What if tragedy strikes? What if it happens to you?

Personalization: Thinking that everything people do or say is some kind of reaction to you. You also compare yourself to others, trying to determine who's smarter, better-looking, etc.

Shoulds: You have a list of ironclad rules about how you and other people should act. People who break the rules anger you and you feel guilty if you violate the rules.

Being Right: You are continually on trial to prove that your opinions and actions are correct. Being wrong is unthinkable and you will go to any length to demonstrate your rightness.

This single page not only explained how I was keeping myself upset; it was the first practical tool that seemed tailored to me, something that could possibly turn my life around. I could learn to think more rationally, less in the extreme and the negative, to think less catastrophic thoughts, to not take everything so personally, and to not take myself so seriously.

In a nutshell, I could replace each twisted thought with the truth!

Untwisting your thinking.

Here are some suggestions on how you can apply this same information. **When you realize that you are becoming agitated (anxious, fearful, hurt, frustrated, or angry), ask yourself, "What was I just thinking?"** Your thoughts may be readily detectable, or they may have been so fleeting, subtle, or ingrained that you were not aware of them. Try to determine exactly what they were. Then check to see if you were being unnecessarily extreme or inappropriately negative. **Being negative is not the same as being realistic**. Did you assume or expect something which is improbable or which singles you out or exaggerates your own importance? Does the evidence support your thoughts?

For example, you may be assuming that the worst is always going to happen to you. Why the worst? Why to you? And if it did happen to you, would it really be able that terrible? Or could you survive it, with God's help and your own and others' resources? **I had been expecting that the worst would happen to me more than to other people, that greater demands would be placed on me than on other people, and that I would be less able to cope than other people would. Does this sound like you? This particular line of thinking offers several possible points for change.**

Learn to ask yourself if you are over-using the words "always" and "never." Are you as aware of the good possibilities as you are of the bad ones? Do you allow yourself to find as much satisfaction in your positive traits and experiences as you find distress in the negative ones?

Are you being unreasonably hard on yourself and others? If you have too many "should's," or unrealistic ones, for yourself, you are a breeding ground for depression and low self-esteem. If you have excessive or unrealistic expectations for others, you will inevitably feel angry, resentful, or hurt a good portion of the time, because you will believe that people are continually letting you down.

In case you think I am underestimating the seriousness of some of the hardships in your life, let me say this: some things ARE catastrophic. But please **save your most extreme reactions for those extreme times**. Also, some rules and expectations ("should's") are good and necessary. The goal here is to be balanced, realistic, and appropriately matter-of-fact.

If you want to learn more about this approach to change, read *Feeling Good: The New Mood Therapy*, by David Burns, a psychiatrist who studied under Aaron Beck. Or read *A New Guide to Rational Living* by Albert Ellis and Robert A. Harper. My dad sent me this book in the summer of 1985 because it had made such a difference in his life. I also found it helpful.

Albert Ellis explains the thought-feeling connection using an A-B-C model. A is the **A**ctivating event, B is the **B**elief (or thought or assumption), and C is the Emotional **C**onsequence. **By changing point B – that is, by changing our thoughts regarding whatever has occurred or may occur – we can achieve a different outcome, a different emotion or degree of emotion at C.** Actually, Ellis continues this process of change with **D**isputing your Thoughts (D) and a new **E**motional Consequence (E). **The questions I suggested above will facilitate your challenging or disputing of B and your substituting a more appropriate thought.**

The Ellis and Burns books will help you examine not only your automatic thoughts but also your underlying belief system, a more subtle set of ideas and assumptions that may be undermining your mental health. [As a Christian, I disagree with Ellis as to whether one of his "irrational" beliefs is entirely faulty or self-defeating, but in general I found the book illuminating. Newer material on false assumptions is available by Christian authors, notably *The Lies We Believe* and *The Truths We Must Believe*, both by Chris Thurman, and *False Assumptions* by Henry Cloud and John Townsend.]

I would tackle my belief system several months later, but for now, I aimed at becoming more aware of my spontaneous cognitions and changing them. I could see that when I had

begun using positive self-talk in order to cope, and examining the "evidence," I was on the right track. Now I had further guidelines to help me "stop worrying."

God said it first.

Apparently my discovery that your thoughts are directly related to the rest of your life was not really a discovery at all, at least as far as the human race is concern. Proverbs 23:7 says, "As he [a man] thinks within himself, so he is," (*NAS*) Jesus himself said, "The good man brings good things out of the good stored up in his heart, and the evil man brings evil things out of the evil stored up in his heart. For out of the overflow of his heart his mouth speaks" (Lk. 6:45). In more than one passage, **Jesus explains that acts of lust and adultery proceed from what is in one's "heart."**

The Apostle Paul therefore encourages us to **"Take captive every thought to make it obedient to Christ"** (2 Cor. 10:5b). **Thoughts may come to us unbidden, but we can choose what to accept, what to discard and which kinds of thoughts we want to nurture in our souls and spirits.**

So what is acceptable food for thought? In **Philippians 4:8**, Paul suggests: "Whatever is true, whatever is noble, whatever is right, whatever is pure, whatever is lovely, whatever is admirable - if anything is excellent or praiseworthy - think about such things."

From the secular world, consider the lyrics to "My Favorite Things": "When the dog bites, when the bee stings, when I'm feeling bad, I simply remember my favorite things, and then I don't feel so bad." Maria leads into this song with these words, "If anything bothers me and I'm feeling unhappy, I just try and think of nice things. Daffodils, green meadows...." **This is cognitive theory in a nutshell: change how you think and you**

will change how you feel. This latter change may happen immediately, or it may take place gradually as your PATTERNS or habits of thinking become more sound.

In *How to Win Over Depression*, Tim LaHaye writes, "Since feelings are caused by the mind, depression must be initiated by a mental thought pattern. Instead of treating the results or symptoms...., **we may confer lifelong relief only through a change in one's thinking pattern.**"

As I reflected on Philippians 4:8, it seemed at first that to follow this advice was something like cheating. That is, to stop or avert distressing thoughts merely by diverting my attention to other thoughts seemed like a cheap short-cut to feeling better. **I guess I was mistakenly figuring that anything constructive had to be more complicated than this**. Also, my overly-serious mind wondered if distraction was too frivolous for God's taste, or if diversion was not just another kind of avoidance.

However, I decided to be practical: if distracting myself mentally and physically helped, then it was worth doing. Focusing on the positive is entirely acceptable as long as you are also examining the deeper issues at appropriate times and in proper balance. Nature does abhor a vacuum. If you attempt to evacuate the negative thoughts without replacing them with something positive, then you are not likely to succeed. **Perhaps thinking about good things needed to become a way of life for me, not just a technique for coping when I was in a pinch, and not just a "distraction."**

About this same time, I was also returning to the idea that, if we are going to think about good things, we should be thanking God for them. The fictional character Pollyanna has been much maligned because of her sugary-sweet philosophy of life, but I believe her perspective has merit. She liked to play what she and her father called the Glad Game, a game that "helps sometimes when things aren't going so well." Her missionary father had pointed out to her that the Bible contains 800 "glad passages" or "happy texts," such as "Shout for joy" and "Be glad in the Lord." Pollyanna asserted to the sour adults around her that **"If God took the trouble to tell us 800 times to be glad and rejoice, He must have wanted us to do it."** I agree.

Additional tips for avoiding worry:

If you have been worrying because of a belief that to NOT worry will somehow increase the risk of things going wrong (because you didn't take them seriously enough), remind yourself that worrying also involves risk. It can consume you and affect your life in a destructive way, as it did mine. **Worrying is just as dangerous as not worrying**, and it is not profitable.

Know that **it is possible to "Be Prepared"** (the Girl Scout and Boy Scout motto) without worrying. It is also possible to be concerned, conscientious, and caring without worrying. Pray and plan, but don't worry.

Pray and practice the Serenity Prayer by Reinhold Niebuhr. Here it is in its entirety:

> God grant me serenity to accept the things I
> cannot change, courage to change the things
> I can and wisdom to know the difference:
> living one day at a time, enjoying one moment
> at a time: accepting hardship as a pathway to
> peace: taking, as Jesus did, this sinful world
> as it is, not as I would have it: trusting that
> You will make all things right if I surrender
> to Your will: so that I may be reasonably
> happy in this life and supremely happy with
> You forever in the next. AMEN

Do not try to control what you cannot control; and do not obsessively try to problem-solve when it is not within your power to solve the problem. Let God be God. **Allow yourself to find relief in the awareness that you are not God and are not supposed to be.** If that knowledge can sink all the way down to your toes, you will experience a new freedom.

For you to ponder:

When I was a patient, I had only the Bible and Leo Buscaglia's book at my fingertips. Over the next few months and years I read voraciously, and discovered many inspirational pearls of wisdom. Here are a few on the subject of thoughts and attitude:

From Epictetus, a first-century Stoic philosopher, in his *Enchiridion*: **"Men feel disturbed not by things, but by the views which they take of them."**

From Steven Biko, a human rights activist in South Africa in the 1970's, as quoted in the movie *Cry Freedom*: **"Change the way people think, and things will never be the same."**

From pastor and author Chuck Swindoll:

> The longer I live, the more I realize the impact of attitude on life. Attitude, to me, is more important than facts.....It will make or break a company...a church...a home. The remarkable thing is **we have a choice every day regarding the attitude we will embrace for the day**. We cannot change our past... we cannot change the fact that people will act in a certain way. We cannot change the inevitable. The only thing we can do is play on the one thing we have, and that is our attitude. I am convinced that **life is 10% what happens to me and 90% how I react to it.**

These lines remind me of the Rockome Gardens sign.

Arm yourself with truth.

Satan knows the importance of the mind; it is his primary battleground. As the father of lies, he deceives, confuses, and tempts, all in the mind. Even physical urges cannot sway you unless your mind concedes. **As warriors for Christ, we must not surrender the ground of our minds to Satan.**

As I began a list of things that would help me avoid worry, I turned back to the Bible. In fact, I wondered if I had done a disservice to God's Word. Perhaps I had discounted important passages just because I wasn't getting what I wanted and thought I needed. **Perhaps there were things between its covers that could help me re-program my mind – ideas or at least incentives.**

Jesus's own words support this concept. He told the believing Jews, "If you hold to my teaching, you are really my disciples. Then you will know the truth, and **the truth shall set you free**" (Jn. 8:31-32). Jesus promised to send the disciples "another Counselor to be with you forever - the Spirit of truth" (Jn. 14:16-17). He said that this Spirit "will guide you into all truth" (Jn. 16:12). Evidently truth is a priority with God.

I assumed, and still do, that Jesus was primarily referring to the truth that leads to salvation, that is, to himself as "the way, the truth, and the life" (John 14:6), but I could also see that there was something healing about all truth. Whether that was truth about my own condition, or truth about what I could reasonably expect from other people, or spiritual realities such as heaven and accountability and sin – I was beginning to experience new freedom and control over my own life as I faced these. I could certainly see that avoiding truth and reality had been detrimental to me.

113

I decided I would avail myself of a variety of resources. **I would re-program my mind with truth, whatever that might entail.** "The discerning heart seeks knowledge" (Prov. 15:14a), and Proverbs 23:12 advises, "Apply your heart to instruction and your ears to words of knowledge." I would **especially pursue Biblical knowledge.** I asked God to cause His words to sink deep into my mind and spirit. I would follow the admonition to "guard my teachings as the apple of your eye. Bind them on your fingers; write them on the table of your heart. Say to wisdom, 'You are my sister,' and call understanding your kinsman" (Prov. 7:2b-4).

Psalm 119:11 says "I have hidden your word in my heart that I might not sin against you." I was realizing that to have God's Word deeply woven into my very being would not only deter me from sin, as the verse said. It would also lead me to peace and a sound mind and more abundant living.

This means that another answer to the question of what is good or acceptable to think about is God's Word itself. You can meditate on specific verses or passages. To be able to do this when the Bible is not at hand, you will need to memorize some passages or at least read scripture frequently enough that the Holy Spirit can bring something to your remembrance. He cannot help you recall something you haven't been exposed to in the first place.

I have never regretted my decision to make truth and God's Word priorities in my life, because they have made such a difference. In fact, I can go even farther and say that the amount of progress which my own clients make is directly proportional to the degree to which they accept truth, reality, and responsibility and avoid lies, half-truths, and secrets.

Chapter 16

But God, You Said....

Several of us, with a therapist in tow, went on an outing one Saturday to a classy mall. We were required to stay in a group as we moved from shop to shop so the therapist could keep an eye on us. I imagined that we looked like a gaggle of geese, or one of those literal chains of kindergartners on a field trip, except that we were not physically bound together. One of the stores carried Christmas potpourri, and the aroma of cinnamon and orange was enchanting. I enjoyed browsing and eating fudge. I wanted to gobble up a half-pound but didn't dare.

We also took a trip to a quaint and artsy part of the city to soak up the atmosphere. Some of the shops sported a Victorian flair and were even located in Victorian homes. I enjoyed the Christmas scents here, too, and the decorations and the specialty ice cream. Except for the hospital bracelets on our wrists, we looked almost normal; I felt more normal, or certainly less abnormal.

Mama, Joe, and David drove up to spend Thanksgiving with me. We played card games in the hospitality suite; I was no good at Hearts. My ability to enjoy the game was compromised by guilty feelings and by my concern that I had not improved more by now. What was I doing here, away from my own family on a major holiday? Joe suggested that I call the boys, but I still was not sure I could handle it. I was doing better, but I thought I might disintegrate when I heard their voices on the phone, and again I was concerned about what that would do to them. On Friday or Saturday I directed Mama, Joe, and David to the site of my most recent outing; I wanted to share the sights and sounds with them. I enjoyed the day to a certain extent.

What about God's promises?

In spite of some improvement, a heavy, unresolved matter hung over my head. I felt I had to come to terms with it, so one day I sat on my bed, resolved not to get up until something was settled. Though Dana and I got along just fine, it was a blessing that she was never in our room when I needed quiet time.

The issue was God – was He there or not? Was He the God I had read and heard about all my life? The God I had believed in all my life? Did He care about me at all? Was He involved in my life or was I on my own? When I had sat at my own piano and given everything up to God, I was confident that He was listening. Now I wasn't so sure.

I was aggravated that He had not answered my requests for healing. Though some of my prayers probably included intercessions on behalf of my family, I mostly prayed to feel better. I had prayed this for months now, and any answers that I could see were meager and slow in forthcoming. Any changes I was making were so small and recent as to seem tenuous; I did not feel like I was solidly on the road to anywhere.

I had a written list of Bible promises that pertained to healing and to receiving what we ask for in prayer. I even had all the conditions written down, such as praying with a believing heart and praying in accordance with God's will. I can see now that my prayers were selfish and short-sighted, but at the time I was in a real spiritual crisis. I held this list out before God and asked if He really meant these promises. I felt like Jacob wrestling with the angel in the book of Genesis.

Wrestling with God.

My thoughts progressed through a certain sequence. I remember it because it was such an important and emotional moment for me.

116

"I am supposed to be able to trust these promises because they are in the Bible. The Bible has assured me that God is trustworthy, that He answers fervent prayer. But I don't see or feel God at work, so is the Bible wrong? Is He not trustworthy?"

I continued my reflection. "Can I trust, as the Sunday School song says, that certain things are true just because 'the Bible tells me so'? The Bible is a remarkable book. It holds together awfully well considering the number of authors and centuries spanned by its writing. Either it is inspired by God or it isn't..... Now I'm back to the matter of faith. I guess this is why they call it faith rather than knowledge. Intellectually speaking, I cannot 'know' for certain that the Bible is anything special, or that God is real. Nobody can 'prove' this to me." I was stumped. I wanted to stamp my foot on the floor in exasperation.

"I will have to trust God's power and love without any convincing evidence. Well, how about the resurrection? Isn't that convincing enough? But the resurrection story we know only from the Bible, and how do I know the Bible is reliable?" Round and round I went. How frustrating.

"What if I assume that the Bible is NOT dependable? There goes the main resource for re-programming my sick mind." That was a disturbing thought. I needed a solid foundation on which to build a healthier mind, and I was not aware of any resource that I could substitute if the Bible wasn't it.

"I guess I don't have anything to lose by trusting the Bible," I thought. "Do I have anything to lose by trusting God?" Same answer. "I might not get better, but if I refrain from trusting, I probably won't get any better either."

So I spoke directly to God: "Okay, God. You are not making this easy, that is if you are really there. But here's what I'm going to do. I am going to trust that you are there

and that you are the loving, powerful Creator I have believed in up to now. I accept this fully, and I will not allow frustrations or unanswered questions to interfere with my faith. I trust myself completely into your hands for you to heal me or do whatever you will with me. I am going to assume that these people and CTU's resources are being provided for me by you and that you intend for me to benefit. If this works and my life is different, I will praise you for the rest of my life. If not, oh well... what have I got to lose?" I was too much in earnest to be amused by how unprayerful this prayer was.

Some illumination at last....

I can't say that I felt better immediately, but God did honor my step of faith before I had even moved away from the bed. Here is what He showed me: **if real faith is not based on feelings or tangible proof, then neither is hope. I could instantly see that if all the things I was prepared to accept as true were in fact true, then there was hope for me whether I could feel it or prove it or not.**

Another truth was illuminated for me also. I had been exposed to "name it, claim it" theology and had apparently bought into it more than I realized. I had seen God as somebody I could manipulate into making life easy and smooth (and to think I had faulted John for this same kind of thinking!) - somebody who would give me whatever I wanted. I had thought the Bible's promises about prayer guaranteed that. Suddenly it hit me: **Faith is not trusting God so much that I believe He will give me whatever I want; faith is trusting God so much that I will do whatever He wants!** Wow! I was almost excited. This was revolutionary.

I was moving closer to the faith of Shadrach, Meshach, and Abednego, who expressed great confidence in God just before

118

they were thrown into the fiery furnace. They told King Nebuchadnezzar,

> "If we are thrown into the blazing furnace,
> the God we serve is able to save us from it,
> and he will rescue us from your hand, O King.
> But even if he does not, we want you to know,
> O King, that we will not serve your gods or
> worship the image of gold you have set up."
> (Dan. 3:17-18)

I had not been spared the fiery furnace, but I found I could exercise faith in God while I was still in it. Even Job's faith eventually became more believable to me. Job said, **"Though he slay me, yet will I hope in him"** (Job 13:15a).

Stepping out in faith.

As you can tell by now, I enjoy movies - not only for their entertainment value, but also for the illustrations they provide. Jesus taught with parables; I like to use stories from movies, knowing that many adults will have seen them. Movies can be an excellent source for quotes of simple wisdom and common sense, as well as for metaphors.

In *Indiana Jones and the Last Crusade,* Indy is faced with a chasm to cross. To accomplish his mission, he must get across, but there is no bridge. Knowing that he is in a spiritual undertaking (of sorts) and that the unexpected may happen, he steps out over the vast, empty darkness. As he leans forward, a bridge appears directly beneath his extended foot. This scene makes a valid point: **we may not see what we are looking for until AFTER we have stepped out in faith.**

In another movie, this time a goofy one, *The Santa Clause,* Scott Calvin says to the elf Judy, as he gazes out over the North

Pole, "I see it, but I don't believe it." Judy responds, "You're missing the point..... **Seeing isn't believing; believing is seeing."** Bingo. Truth is truth, even when it comes from Balaam's donkey.

God did do awesome things in my life, and I praise Him for it. I encourage you to trust Him completely. Read Psalm 34:18, "The Lord is close to the brokenhearted and saves those who are crushed in spirit." **Trust that God is with you whether you FEEL His presence or not.** "Where can I go from your Spirit: where can I flee from you presence? If I go up to the heavens, you are there; **if I make my bed in the depths, you are there**" (Ps. 139:7-8).

A new promise.

The irony of my spiritual crisis was that every single day God had been speaking to me clearly. I went to the hospital chapel at least once a day to pray and meditate. I liked the quietness and the ever-burning candle. Mostly I just sensed in my desperation that this was the best place to turn. Every time I sat down in a pew, I "heard" in my head the distinct message, **"Many people will benefit from your experience."**

I did not hear what I wanted to hear, which was that I would get better myself. The one message was repeated and was always the same. One day the impression of a crowd of people (I assumed these were the ones who were to "benefit") was so strong that I turned to see if there were people pressing in behind me. The chapel looked empty as always, but apparently God was there. I did not "hear voices." I simply heard God.

Why did this daily experience not strengthen my faith? Because I felt so bad that the very idea of me helping anybody was laughable, even though I didn't feel like laughing. My mood and my anxiety created a wall that was nearly impervious to a number of good things, including this promise.

Yet the message did eventually inspire hope in me, as it dawned on me that if God was going to use me to help people, I would have to be in reasonably good shape, certainly in better condition than I was in at the time. Obviously God was involved in my life, but this did not stop me from challenging Him when my feelings were so slow to change. I believe He was also trying to encourage me to be more selfless in my thinking and praying. I was slow to catch on.

Has God been trying to show you something and you have almost missed it because it is not what you are looking for? Is it possible He has been at work, for example, in encouraging phone calls or words of advice, and you have not recognized Him? Maybe you have tried to box God in as I did. Be sure you look at all the evidence for God's involvement in your life; **don't mistakenly assume that He isn't doing anything just because you don't feel better first. Give God a chance to implement His plan; after all, yours has probably not worked.**

Recovery requires active surrender.

One of the ongoing balancing acts I undertook was the partnership between God and myself: learning how to let God do His part in my recovery while I did my part. I had learned not to expect other people to fix me, but to what extent was God going to fix me? How much of this was up to me? **When I made my peace with Him that day, I was engaging in what I would call active surrender.** I surrendered my need to call the shots and to have all my doubts addressed, but I did not become passive. I continued my efforts to do my part in helping myself, because I believed the tools I was being given were provided by God.

If this seems strange to you, reflect on **John 9:6-11**. On this occasion, Jesus does not heal merely with a touch or by the spoken word. He makes mud out of dirt and saliva, puts it on the man's eyes, and then tells him to go wash it off in the pool of Siloam. **If the man had not done his part, he would have remained blind**. It was not only okay that he took action himself; he was being obedient in doing so. Often, surrendering means taking action - action under God's direction.

I share this story so you will know that while you need to look to God as your Healer, you may be called upon to participate in your own recovery. The fact that you are reading this book suggests that you believe you are to do so. Pray that God will give you discernment as to where your responsibility begins and ends. If He wants you only to pray and wait, do so. If He wants you to do something more, do it. If you make mistakes, thank God for His grace and forgiveness!

Your faith and your intellect are both important.

You may be confused on a certain point by now. I explained in Chapter 15 how important it was for me to guard and train my mind, because my mind was such a key to recovery. Now I have told you in this chapter that some things cannot be accomplished with your mind; you must reach out in your spirit and accept some things on faith, whether or not your mind concurs.

Both of these points are "truths." The tricky part -- and again you must count on God's Holy Spirit to help you with this - is in discerning which is relevant in a given situation. **Spiritual truths cannot be arrived at intellectually. Yet other things must be comprehended and processed in the mind; you cannot untwist your distorted thinking without involving your mind**. Our minds and spirits are intricately bound up in these bodies of ours, and it is important that we be good stewards of both, and allow Jesus to be the Lord of both.

The book of Hebrews explains why faith is called just that: "Now faith is being sure of what we hope for and certain of what we do not see" (11:1). That same chapter commends a multitude of Old Testament heroes for their faith. God is looking for faith in you and me. Remember my saying that I had to accept responsibility for my own recovery, NO MATTER WHAT? **The same principle applies with faith; God asks us to trust Him NO MATTER WHAT**. No conditions. In fact, Hebrew 11:6 says that "without faith it is impossible to please God."

If you continue to doubt God...

God will help you remove the stumbling blocks to recovery, if you don't get in His way, and if you don't balk when He gives you something to do. If you have read this, and after considering it, you find that you are still disappointed in God or doubting Him, seek out one of these books: *When God Doesn't Make Sense* by James Dobson or *Disappointment With God* by Philip Yancey. Both books are excellent.

If you read these and still feel hopeless or dissatisfied, perhaps you have some deep pain related to earlier trauma or abuse. For example, you may find it virtually impossible to see God as a trustworthy heavenly Father if you were abused by your own earthly father. **Please locate a dependable, compassionate counselor who will help you work through these things**. Some pain must be brought out into the light of Truth and the light of Jesus's love and be faced squarely before you can let go of it.

Once you have done this, begin the process of forgiveness. If you try to speak words of forgiveness too quickly, you may discover that these are lip service only and that resentment still festers. But do let go as you are able.

Keep in mind that forgiveness is not saying that the wrong never occurred, or that it occurred but wasn't wrong, or that it wasn't painful. If you stop and consider it, forgiveness is something which by necessity is done only when a sin or wrong

123

has been committed, otherwise why would there be a need to forgive?

God knows what the offender has done in your life and will hold him or her accountable if there is no genuine repentance in that person. God can avenge and vindicate in a way which will out-do anything you could do, if such is called for. You can let go of the need to even the score or even to have that individual restore something to you. While it may appear that forgiving means that you are letting the person off the hook, in reality it is you that will be released. As long as you harbor a grudge or keep waiting for something which may not ever be delivered to you, you stayed tied to the other person in your heart. You can release yourself by forgiving.

And "forgive" God for whatever He has permitted that you don't understand. If God did not explain Himself to Job, He is probably not going to give account to you. However, notice that God did eventually restore everything to Job, and there is a restoration ahead for you. Job's restoration occurred after he was able to let God off the hook, revere God as God, and pray for his offending friends.

If you are not a survivor of abuse or trauma, yet are bogged down with doubts and frustration with God, then I strongly suggest that you step out in faith in spite of yourself. Ask God to show you what your hang-up is and how to address it, but don't sit around indefinitely waiting for an answer. While you sit back, you suffer. Make a move, then perhaps the desired feelings or answers will come to you.

Catch the hope contained in the following verses: "Now to **him who is able to do immeasurably *more* than all we can ask or imagine, according to his power that is at work *within* us,** to him be glory in the church and in Christ Jesus throughout all generations, for ever and ever! Amen." (Eph. 3:21-22).

Chapter 17

I Don't Feel Like It!

I reached a point where my feelings were more normal – that is, I experienced some positive feelings again, and my emotional reactions seemed more appropriate. I have mentioned that I enjoyed our outings and meals. I began to find pleasure in working with colors and designs in expressive therapy. When I walked in the garden on a sunny day, I could almost sense God's presence again. John brought my pillow from home, and I was pleasantly surprised at what a difference this made. It smelled like home, and my sense that I was in another world almost completely dissipated when I hugged my pillow to me.

I was still shaky, but this seemed to represent a surface nervousness more than the deep-seated anxiety I had been burdened with for so long. My mood was definitely brighter.

It's time to address the subject of feelings, a big topic with several facets. If you are like I was, your feelings have owned you for quite some time, and now you are struggling to get a perspective on them. I have learned much about my emotions, beginning with my experience in St. Mark's.

Don't give your feelings too much credit.

The first point you may have guessed, if you followed me through the last chapter. And that is that **when it comes to matters of faith and hope, feelings do not provide a good plumb line.** Feelings can be blown hither and yon by too many different forces. Because of this, **they are also not a solid foundation for determining truth.**

One of the cognitive fallacies described on our Beck handout **was called emotional reasoning**, which basically means that you make **the mistake of assuming that your feelings represent how things really are. It would be incorrect to reason that if you feel worthless you must be worthless, or if you feel guilty you are definitely guilty, or if you feel God has vanished then He necessarily has done so.** Yet many of us have made these errors in reasoning.

In other matters, such as making decisions, large and small, feelings also are not trustworthy as a guideline, or at least not as a solitary guideline. I began to learn this before any such premise was ever stated, when I was required to do the same activities as the other patients without regard to how I felt. If I had postponed attending group until I felt cordial and confident, or taking medication until I felt stronger, or participating in expressive therapy until my hands stopped shaking and the songs didn't seem too sad - I would have had an unnecessarily long stint at St. Mark's.

The principle of not using feelings as a guideline for behavior is incorporated into two GROW sayings: **"I can compel my muscles and limbs to act rightly in spite of my feelings," and "I will go by what I know, not by how I feel." Powerful.**

At home, before I was admitted to St. Mark's, I had let my feelings be my criteria for everything; if I didn't feel like doing something, I didn't do it. Work didn't get done, my whole family suffered, and I had fewer and fewer accomplishments to feel good about.

Remember George Banks from the movie *Mary Poppins*? Mr. Banks calls the police station to ask for a constable to help find his lost children. In his agitation and haste, he fails to notice that the children have appeared in the doorway. When Winifred tries

126

to get his attention, George responds, "Kindly do not attempt to cloud the issue with facts!"

Have you somehow come to regard facts as irrelevant, because you place so much stock in your feelings? Perhaps it's time to give facts their proper due and not let your judgment be clouded by your feelings. **If you have been making most of your decisions on the basis of emotion or mood, it's time to stop.**

You can do it!

It is also possible that you have based too many choices on how you feel physically. Depression may cause you to feel tired, but that does not mean that what you actually need is rest, or that you will feel better if you have rested. **So ask yourself during a given hour or morning, what would I do right now if I didn't feel this way? Answer yourself, and then do these things in spite of how you feel.** Of course if you have a physical condition that prohibits normal activity, disregard the above. What I want you to do is to **overcome the illusion (created by depression and anxiety) that you cannot do anything.**

I understand that depression causes you to feel that you're in a Catch-22 situation: the things you should do in order to feel better you "can't" do because you don't feel better. Barbara Johnson, a Christian humorist, shares some of her favorite bumper-sticker slogans in two delightful books (listed in the reference section). One of these stickers conveys what this inertia feels like: "I'm really not in good enough shape to get in shape right now." Though the reference was probably to physical fitness, it also applies to mental and emotional fitness.

A charming song in Disney's animated *Robin Hood* also does justice to this condition. The king's subjects who were unable to pay their taxes have been thrown in jail, and the minstrel (in the voice of Roger Miller) sings to them:

> Every town has its ups and downs.
> Sometimes ups outnumber the downs,
> but not in Nottingham.
> I'm inclined to believe,
> *if we weren't so down,*
> *we'd up and leave.*
> *We'd up and fly if we had wings for flying.*
> Can't you see the tears we're crying?
> Can't there be some happiness for me?
> Not in Nottingham.

Try breaking out of your inertia and the "I-can't-do-it" mindset. Put forth the effort to do something normal or constructive or selfless. Except for the effort, the cost probably will not be high, and you may even benefit, especially once you get back into the habit of doing things. You can do the "ordinary" thing in spite of how you feel (remember the Principle of Ordinariness?).

Pain is not the enemy.

The CTU program had its own theme or motto which was changed every few months. The refrain I heard throughout my stay was **"No pain, no gain."** I hated it at first. I was here because I wanted to be FREE from pain, not because I was looking for more. Now I was being told that pain was necessary or even good. The only way to recover or grow, i.e., to "gain," was through pain, effort, perseverance, and sacrifice.

I made my way through a process of merely accepting or tolerating pain - a neutral approach - to a place where I could see that suffering is partly the means by which God molds us - a positive approach. I did not arrive at that perspective overnight. Over the next few years I would continue to expand my understanding of suffering, some of which I will share in Chapter 20, but for now I offer this simple lesson from **the Old Testament image of a potter at work. Pressure, heat, and time are necessary for a final product of quality. If you allow God to mold you through these, you will be a fine vessel. If, on the other hand, you avoid pain and discomfort at all cost, you risk staying sick and not as usable as God desires you to be.** In addition, as GROW says, "the more I run away from suffering and need to avoid it, the less it will take to torment me."

Act as if....

A principle common to a number of recovery programs is the "act as if" philosophy. **What this means is that you determine what your behavior would be if your problem had vanished, and then practice that behavior.** For example, the depressed person can deliberately engage in the behaviors she would do if she were not depressed. At first glance, to "act as if you were well" or "act as if you were happy" sounds like hypocrisy. I am not suggesting hypocrisy, because truth and honesty are crucial.

Let me help you distinguish between being hypocritical and following the above principle. The intent of hypocrisy is deception; the intent of "acting as if" is to retrain the body and mind to behave and think in healthy ways - to build in wholesome habits. Hypocrisy may involve a lack of self-awareness or the avoidance of facing issues in one's self; the healthy principle encourages the person to be self-aware and to work on issues, but to move ahead behaviorally without waiting for perfect insight or resolution on every issue. Some people express the "act as if" philosophy with the saying, "Fake it till you make it." The meaning is the same; don't let the word "fake" confuse you.

One of the ways I gained control during my panic attacks was to try to guard my facial expression, speech, and posture so that I would not even give away that I was having a panic attack; I was "acting as if" I were calm on the inside. Training myself to do this actually did help me become more calm and composed.

Stop waiting until you feel totally together before you do the "together" thing. You cannot learn everything you need to learn while sitting on the sidelines. The only way to learn to ride a bike is to ride one; the only way to learn to ski is to ski; you can't really learn to live unless you go ahead and live. Another of Barbara Johnson's bumper stickers comes to mind: "Smile. It kills time between disasters." You can manage a reasonably pleasant demeanor even if you do not feel buoyant or giddy. Consider it "happiness practice."

Don't put the keys to your contentment in someone else's hands.

The next aspect of feelings I had to learn is this: who is responsible for my feelings? I am. Who is responsible for your feelings? You are. This was a hard concept for me to learn, because it was so easy to place the blame for my bad feelings on other people's remarks and behavior, or on the circumstances. However, realizing that the responsibility lies in my hands means, as I said earlier, that no other human being can steal my happiness, any more than he or she can give it to me.

In case you don't grasp this, remember the A-B-C model. **Between every event (or remark or stressor) and your emotion, there is a thought. Because you have the opportunity to determine what the thought is at point B - or to change it if you don't like what pops into your head - you also have the opportunity to influence the emotional outcome at point C. You can determine how upset you become by what you tell yourself.**

130

Of course, as a human being, you are going to be affected by people and situations; it is natural to feel grief over a loss and jubilation over a triumph. It is likely that certain things will trigger certain feelings. However, **if you accept responsibility for your thoughts and feelings, you can limit the DEGREE to which your emotional buttons get pushed**. You don't have to be yanked around like a yo-yo. You can acquire more stability and reduce the duration and frequency of extreme mood swings.

Nobody can make you feel anything. If you can really accept this, then you can move out of a victim mentality. You may still have preferences, for example, that an abrasive friend would treat you with more consideration, but you do not have to let her every word or action injure you. Your own mental response can provide a buffer for your heart.

If you tell yourself, "It's positively awful that she treats me this way. She should know better, and I shouldn't have to put up with this," you are going to feel angry or resentful and possibly even withdraw from a relationship that is worth keeping. On the other hand, you could tell yourself, "I wish she would be more sensitive, but I can accept her because she is a good friend." This way you will be merely disappointed. Or you might think, "I'll tell her how I feel, because she truly may not know," then you can express yourself to her assertively (not aggressively). Rational thinking not only helps you control your emotions; it also makes your communication more effective.

Also, guard against an over-active imagination and mind-reading. I would learn later in GROW that my emotions do not distinguish between imaginings and thoughts of something real; my feelings will be equally responsive to either. Therefore, if I want my emotions to be appropriate, healthy, and reasonably positive, I should not be fueling them by assuming and expecting the worst when the truth or reality of a situation may not be that bad.

One day when I was reading the Bible in my hospital room, I came across Paul's words in Philippians 4:12: **"I have learned the secret of being content in any situation....." This became a goal for me. If I could learn to control my emotions and not let my buttons get pushed, perhaps I could accomplish this. I definitely wanted contentment.**

I was pleased to note that living above the circumstances was a learning process for Paul and not something he accomplished overnight. I still have not become a master at this, but I have come a long way. Here are some of the things I learned to do to foster contentment in myself:

1) **Apply Paul's next verse, "I can do everything through him [Christ] who gives me strength."** Nobody can take him away from you.

2) **Have realistic expectations and process things rationally**, in keeping with the goal of "renewing my mind."

3) **Forgive old hurts and continue to forgive as new offenses occur.**

4) **Allow God to be your source of happiness and health as well as strength.** "Thou wilt keep him in perfect peace whose mind is stayed on thee" (Isa. 26:3, *KJV*). Meditate on God himself, or on Christ, who told his disciples, "Peace I leave with you; my peace I give you. I do not give to you as the world gives. Do not let your hearts be troubled and do not be afraid" (Jn. 14:27).

The fruit of the Holy Spirit - which is the spirit of the risen Christ - includes peace, a peace that does not depend on peaceful circumstances. Jesus was promising peace in the midst of a discourse in which he also promised perse-cution and tribulation in this world.

If you are going to experience this kind of peace, you must stop expecting the world to deliver it to you. God's peace comes from the permanently indwelling Holy Spirit; worldly peace comes from temporary things and fickle people, and you will never be able to get everything and everybody to cooperate with you at the same time. **Give up the conditional "I'll be fine when...." Be fine** *in* - **in Jesus.**

Gary Smalley taught along these same lines in the *Love Is a Decision* Seminar which he presented with John Trent. He said that most of us want God *plus* something, instead of simply being contented with God. We forget the awesome, miraculous blessing that we have in God, who has graciously saved us from ourselves and lovingly given us a part of Himself. **Be content that your cup is filled by Christ and accept that everything else doesn't matter all that much,** at least not in terms of your own inner peace. Don't expect people, places, and things to fulfill in a way which only Jesus can. This way you won't come unglued when someone or something lets you down. We give others the power to hurt and upset us when we expect something from them, Smalley says. If people do come through for you, allow them to be the "overflow."

In the meantime, stop holding other people responsible for your feelings. I am not saying that hurt isn't real or that it does not matter if you get hurt. I am saying that you can exercise control over the extent to which you feel hurt. Gary Smalley indicates that **accepting responsibility for your own feelings is a sign of maturity.** I recommend leaving the offending person in God's hands; He will hold them accountable for their words and actions.

Don't make happiness your primary goal.

By the time of my hospitalization, I had made happiness a top priority, because I had not felt unequivocally happy in a long time. All happy feelings had been compromised by anxiety. So while we are discussing feelings, I want to share some thoughts on happiness, in case you also long for it. Though I did not find these principles articulated until some time later, I was learning to operate by them when I ceased focusing on my feelings.

GROW says that **I tend to defeat my own purpose when I aim primarily for happiness, but if I strive for something more important, the thing I desire may come my way as a result.** The more I pursue pleasure directly, the more it will elude me, "for either my anxiety to secure it will upset the naturalness of the behaviour that brings it about, or....it will take more and more to satisfy me." Jesus said it first when he said that we should **first seek the kingdom of God and His righteousness, and then "all these things" will come to us** (Mt. 6:33).

Phillip Gulley, a Quaker pastor, makes the same point in a story from his book, *Front Porch Tales*. He says,

> As I've grown older, my understanding of happiness
> has changed. It used to take a new piece of furniture
> to make me happy; now if the boys are healthy and
> Joan and I go to bed sleeping spoons, that's about as
> good as it gets. When it takes less and less to be con-
> tent, we're on our way to joy. I don't want you to get
> the idea that I'm super-holy or anything. **I've just no-
> ticed that people who try hard to be happy seldom
> are.** Besides, happiness based on things is fleeting –
> cars rust, and the cat coughs up a hair ball on the new
> couch. We're better off aiming for peace at the center.*

*Excerpted from *Front Porch Tales*, © 1997 by Philip Gulley. Used by permission of Multnomah Publishers, Inc.

I have referred more than once to the movie *Groundhog Day*, and here I go again. Phil finally finds happiness and contentment when he quits looking for them. In particular, he wins Rita's heart when he gives up feverishly trying to do so. In addition, he gets out of his "stuck" state when he shifts his focus from feeding his appetites and ending his pain to, instead, developing his talents, improving his skills, and serving others. Phil's priority has become "What can I do for you today?" His self-respect and generosity endear him to people in a way his self-indulgence and self-pity never did. He has also learned to make the most of the moment (in a constructive way). This has been an ongoing lesson for me, because I tend to be so forward-looking that I miss the preciousness of today.

In short, if you want to feel good, stop focusing on feeling good. Focus on becoming Christlike, actively loving God and others, thinking straight, and feeding on the Word, and then see what happens.

Should you let your feelings out or hold them in?

I was being told that I should get in touch with my feelings and get them out. At the same time I was clearly being discouraged from expressing everything I felt and from basing my choices on my feelings. This sounds like two contradictory objectives, so I had some sorting out to do.

I have learned that the key is not as simple as just getting emotion out or just holding it in. The key is balance - knowing when to express feelings and when to refrain. GROW says that my feelings are like children in a classroom; I am the teacher who decides which ones get permission to express themselves, and **I have probably been either too lenient or too strict in my control.**

135

If you want to be emotionally healthy and to have appropriately intimate relationships, **you must be able to feel your feelings, to acknowledge and name them (at least some of the time), and to express them in a way that facilitates understanding.** Some individuals are not much aware of what they feel and have to learn to identify their emotions. Others are aware but need to learn how to express themselves more effectively.

On the other hand, some of us have worn our feelings on our sleeves and verbalized every complaint. The challenge for me was in learning not to give too much weight to what I felt and to not share absolutely everything with somebody. **Not every twinge of emotion or discomfort is worth sharing.** I remain more stable emotionally and get along better with others if I air only some things, and I have relied on God to show me when and how to do this.

By the way, almost everyone can benefit from learning better expressive skills. Most people seem to be either too aggressive, too passive, or just plain unclear in what they say.

Also, most of us could improve our listening skills. **Other people will be pleased if you give as much attention to their feelings as you do to your own.** Loving and satisfying relationships include consideration and empathy. Most people "live and breathe" where their emotions are, so you will go far in understanding and interacting with them if you can at least take their feelings into consideration. **You don't have to agree with a person's opinions and beliefs to communicate appreciation, validation, and even empathy for their feelings.**

If you are examining how well you share your emotions with others, take a look at the positive as well as the negative ones. That is, the expressions of anger, hurt, or disappointment should be joined by, and preferably outnumbered by, genuine expressions of love, respect, joy, praise, and gratitude. If you have been thinking negatively, then you have probably been speaking negatively. People get tired of pessimism and whining, doom and gloom. They will appreciate it if you can loosen up your vocal chords and voice some positive things for a change. God will also appreciate it.

In summary, avoid the all-or-nothing approach when it comes to experiencing and expressing feelings. Try not to indulge in the extremes, unless this is truly called for.

Pain that has never seen the light of day is among the emotions which you *should* consider expressing.

As I said in the previous chapter, if you sense that you have old buried pain - repressed or denied emotion - it's probably time to face this and get it out. This is one instance in which feelings should be given the attention they deserve and have been denied until now. Find a way to do this effectively so that you can heal and move on and not wallow around in misery indefinitely. Even if you are not wallowing in misery, your views of yourself, God, and others may be poisoned, and your ability to relate in a genuinely loving manner may be compromised by this old pain. If now is not the time to open up the wounds, then ask God to show you if and when the time is right.

If you decide to seek therapy for longstanding or deep issues, you might appreciate this word of warning: for just a little while you may feel worse before you feel better. An illustration may explain why: when I do a major housecleaning job, such as cleaning out closets or cabinets, I first pull everything out into the open, so that I can dust or wipe thoroughly and see what I am dealing with. However, this procedure creates quite a mess. In the fall of 1996 I undertook (and completed) a

137

major task: going through memorabilia and nostalgic "stuff" from four generations in my family. I got everything out, and my house looked like a flea market for a while, but getting everything out into the open enabled me to decide which items were disposable, which I wanted to store (and how to label and organize them), and which to display.

Similarly, facing memories such as abuse, betrayal, loss, and painful messages is a way of bringing things out into the light and into view. You cannot decide what to trash or sort or treasure with any wisdom or finality until you first face the mess. The understanding you gain should serve you well in terms of inner peace and getting over the stumbling blocks in your life. The pain and chaos will diminish over time, as you finish what you've begun.

Pray for wisdom.

How will you know when to trust your feelings as a guideline? When to express your feelings and when to keep your mouth shut? How will you know the extent to which your past should be dug up? How will you get past the tendencies to blame others for your hurts or to put your own feelings ahead of theirs? With wisdom, the kind that most of us do not have naturally. James 1:5 says, "If any of you lacks wisdom, he should ask God, who gives generously to all without finding fault, and it will be given to him." God may also send wise, mature individuals your way who can help you grow in understanding and in specific applications of these teachings.

Summing it up.

I'll close this chapter with the words to a song which I wrote in 1990. I was wanting to capture the essence of what I had learned during and following my 1984 experience. The song is a prayer of sorts. The heart of the message is in the chorus, which

138

follows each verse. I'm not sure the lyrics are very powerful without the music, but here they are:

Shifting Tides

Vs. 1:
I had hoped I'd never have another day like today.
I'm discouraged and worried, and the blues won't go
  away.
Though you said you're with me always, I don't feel you
  with me now,
But I'm trusting that you'll light my way somehow.

Chorus:
And I'm so glad the Truth does not depend on feeling,
And that you're the same today and evermore.
If you're the Way, the Truth, and Life, then there's
  always hope for me;
In the shifting tides, you're my unchanging shore.

Vs. 2:
I had thought that with your Spirit, I would always feel
  you near.
I would cope with life, feel warm inside, and keep my
  thinking clear.
Though emotion and confusion seem to change the
  facts today,
I guess they're just the shadows life throws in my way.

Chorus again:

Vs. 3:
Though I feel like I'm abandoned, you said you'd hold me
  in your hand.
Though I feel like I am falling, your strength will help me
  stand.

Though the thrill of the mountaintop is just a memory
today,
I know you're just as close in the valleys along the way.

Chorus again:

Vs. 4:
**If faith is more than feeling, then I'll go by what I
know:**
You'll love and never leave me - the Bible tells me so.
And if faith in you grows stronger when the climb is all
uphill,
Then it's time to grow and know you better still.

Chorus again:

Coda: And in the shifting tides I'll cling to your
changeless shore.

Chapter 18

Explain It To Me, Please

I was feeling less distressed all the time and more on an even keel. I was even rediscovering my sense of humor. I played ping-pong with a patient and then, a few days later, after he'd had shock treatments, we played again. I made a reference to our earlier games, which he did not remember playing. Our disjointed conversation was funny, and we were both comically uncoordinated. We couldn't have hit the ball if our lives had depended on it. I assumed this was from our medication. Instead of this being disconcerting to me, as when I had attempted unsuccessfully to play the piano, I found it amusing.

The delusions of a woman on our ward were also rather entertaining. I felt too much compassion and respect for her to laugh aloud, but she did bring a smile to my face. She believed she was a famous male political figure. My ability to be amused by anything was promising.

Are we there yet?

In spite of my progress, I still had a lot of questions. At first I wondered how long I was going to be in St. Mark's and if there was any guarantee that the program and medication would work for me. The stakes for not getting well were awfully high. Then, when I could acknowledge that I was getting better, I wondered if I would be relapse-free and how long I would have to continue the various therapies. "When will I be well?" I wondered. **I wanted a timetable.**

In fact, I wanted to see the whole big picture - what my original problem was, which problems developed as a result of this, and how the puzzle pieces of recovery would fit into one whole picture. Was my unhealthy dependence on people a cause of my disorders or a consequence? What about the negative thinking? And the spiritual uncertainty - did I not trust God enough in the first place, or did my torment result in doubts?

I finally realized that I was not going to know the sequence of things at that time. Either knowing was not important or was not possible for me yet. It was obvious that dependence, negativity, and doubt had to go, no matter when they had entered the picture. It was also obvious that I was beginning to recover even without understanding precisely how I had deteriorated.

I wanted to understand not only how I came to be sick but also exactly how I would get well. I wanted to know what self-esteem and assertiveness had to do with wholeness, and what personality types had to do with mood, and where love and faith and rational thinking fit in with these. Was there some order in which I was to incorporate these things into my life? And how was I doing? I wanted to hear God say, "Now when you have mastered this skill, you will be 20% recovered," or "When you have finished such and such, proceed over here." I like outlines and plans and I wanted to see what God had in mind for me, as well as a clear outline of the steps for accomplishing this.

What I learned was that my life is like a jigsaw puzzle and God holds the lid to the box, so only He can see the final picture. This means that the toughest assembly work is in His hands. I can open the box, take out the pieces (reasoning or faith or communication skills) and become familiar with them, even organizing them and possibly fitting a couple together. God clearly expected me to make use of the pieces (the resources) He had provided, but I cannot assemble or even envision the final product. God does that. We do not have to be able to see what God can see. "Woe to him who quarrels with his Maker, to him

142

who is but a potsherd among the potsherds on the ground. **Does the clay say to the potter, 'What are you making?'"** (Isa. 45:9)

We cannot in fact know everything that God knows, and that is not all bad. Any god that our finite minds could fully comprehend would be a puny god. If I thought that God did not know any more than I did, I would miss the blessing of being able to leave things in His hands and lean on Him for support.

And it's a good thing that I can admit to ignorance; if I thought I understood everything, I would undoubtedly be dangerous to the rest of the world, because I would be mistaken. I would make a lousy god.

God does know more. "The secret things belong to the Lord our God," says Deuteronomy 29:29a. "For my thoughts are not your thoughts, neither are your ways my ways," declares the Lord. "As the heavens are higher than the earth, so are my ways higher than your ways and my thoughts than your thoughts" (Isa. 55:8-9). Proverbs 3:5-6 admonishes us to "Trust in the Lord with all your heart and lean not on your own understanding; in all your ways acknowledge him, and he will make your paths straight."

Tales of God's omniscience.

Philip Gulley writes about the puzzling aspects of life in his book of tales. I like the way he expresses himself. The excerpts below are from two different stories.

> There are some things about this life I'll never understand. One of them is why a drunken driver dies of old age when a never-hurt-a-flea young man barely sees twenty. **Someday, I'm going to see God face to face. And when I do, I'm going to ask Him why that is.**

143

One thing I've never understood is why I'm so blessed - good parents, good wife, good kids, good job - and others aren't. I used to think it was because I was nice to God, until I met some battered saints. Now I just think there's a randomness in this world beyond my understanding. **The apostle Paul said that on this side of things we see in a mirror dimly.***

Even if you do not believe in randomness, I doubt that you personally can make sense of everything that happens.

Surrender some more.

I was able while I was in St. Mark's to relinquish everything into God's hands. I was becoming more matter-of-fact in my approach to things, and I could see that scrambling to be as knowledgeable as God was fruitless. This time I could let go without feeling that something was being wrenched from me. My yielding to God seemed to be occurring in phases.

I like the following poem about surrender. I saw it once on a greeting card and now have it posted on my bulletin board. I do not know who wrote it.

"Let Go and Let God"

As children bring their broken toys
With tears for us to mend,
I brought my broken dreams to God
Because He was my friend.
But, then instead of leaving Him
In peace to work alone,
I hung around and tried to help
With ways that were my own.

*Excerpted from *Front Porch Tales*, © 1997 by Philip Gulley. Used by permission of Multnomah Publishers, Inc.

> At last I snatched them back and cried,
> "How can you be so slow?"
> "My child," He said, "What could I do?
> You never did let go."

Letting go was becoming easier for me. By the way, did you know that the words in Psalm 46:10 which we are accustomed to seeing translated as "be still" or "cease striving" literally mean "*let go, relax*" in the original? The verse makes such sense that way. Knowing that God is who He is, it is easier to put things in His hands and confidently leave them there.

Now what about the time element?

I accepted that it was going to take time to "arrive." Gulley says that each of us are like his kitchen table, which he slowly and carefully crafted himself and lovingly polishes with lemon oil once a week. He makes two good points about his table and the work that went into it: **"doing something worthwhile takes time" and the table is "never really finished. Kind of like me."**

Now that I have been in the counselor role for several years, I better understand God's position as a Counselor. When a client comes to me for help, she is not only asking for assistance; she is also placing her trust in me. However, she forgets this sometimes and wants me to do everything her way. If her way were adequate, she would not have needed to consult me in the first place. Presumably, I am capable of offering her something which she does not have (or is not yet aware of having).

There are times when, in order for the client to "own" her own insight or belief or responsibility, the awareness must come spontaneously from within herself, not from me, and this process cannot be rushed. Some understandings will simply be more fruitful and lasting if they germinate and grow from the inside. That is, sometimes a direct explanation from me will be detrimental because the person must come to see things for herself. Even when direct explanations are not detrimental, they may be futile. **Other times I can plant a seed in the client, so to speak, but I cannot make the idea take root and endure.**

Much recovery is actually growth, which is a process over time, where certain things unfold in a natural sequence, including the appearance of fruit which - as is the case with fruit trees - may not appear for a few seasons. Overnight change would be called "invention" or "magic," but not "growth." The principles I see operating in my clients are the same principles by which God may be working in each of us.

There are additional reasons why the passing of time may be important. As new input gels in the client's head, it may take time for this to be assimilated into her speech and behavior and especially into her very being. Also, it is over time that new behavioral skills and new ways of thinking become familiar and habitual.

When a client becomes exasperated with me and wants me to make things happen faster or make everything crystal-clear, I find myself wanting to respond, "I thought you trusted me." I imagine that God feels this same way when we plead for help and then whine because He doesn't wave a magic wand or explain everything or follow our dictates. God is not codependent. He feels no obligation or compulsion to please or appease us, and He will not be manipulated. Would we want a God who would be, given how misguided our demands and whims can be?

Not only does change take time, but you will probably need to persevere in prayer. In Luke 18 Jesus tells the story of a tenacious widow who pleads with a judge until he finally grants her request. God is like this judge, Jesus says; He rewards persistence. So don't be faint-hearted or impatient. Persevere. Remember that what you have with God is a relationship, and communication is vital to every good relationship. Trust God, but don't take Him for granted.

When God looks at you, He does not nail a "condemned" sign across your forehead. You are not ready for demolition. On the other hand, He also knows that you need more than a quick coat of paint. God sees a fixer-upper in you, and as you know if you have ever re-modeled a house, restoration involves time.

Possible courses of recovery.

The changes I implemented at St. Mark's did not end there. I continued to apply what I'd learned for months and years and, in fact, I use the same principles now. The difference is that now these alterations have become part of who I am, so that much less effort is involved in maintaining mental and emotional health.

You will notice in your own recovery that sometimes you leap ahead, sometimes you take moderate strides or only baby steps, and occasionally you even seem to slip back. This is normal. Also, plateaus are normal. These are times when you consolidate your gains before growing some more. I think I basically plodded along at a steady pace with intermittent plateaus, setbacks, and bursts of momentum.

I like the story of Jesus healing the blind man in Mark 8:22-26. After Jesus had put saliva on the man's eyes and touched him, the man could see people, but they looked "like trees walking around." The man's sight was fully restored only after Jesus touched his eyes a second time. We could debate all day why it took two touches, when on other occasions Jesus healed with only one touch or by the spoken word. We cannot know why this situation was different, but it does tell us something: **God does not heal or restore everyone in the same way, and there may even be periods of time when recovery appears to be stalled.** You may feel like your recovery comes in installments, as the blind man's did, and that's okay. Or you may have a slower, steadier healing, or a more dramatic and immediate one.

You may be wondering **what the difference is between your efforts now and your efforts earlier.** In both situations, you have really tried to get better. First of all, if you have been on the same track as myself, your early efforts were more superficial and possibly too defensive. They were also stemming from your desperation, not from insight and understanding. You may have been earnest but misguided. Or, it is possible that some of what you tried earlier was good but couldn't be effective until you backed it up with a more sound rationale, better motives, and more realistic expectations. Perhaps you have a clearer idea now of what God's part is in your recovery and what is up to you.

If your early efforts to get better mostly proved futile, you may have given up. You may feel that nothing you try is going to make a difference anyway. The lack of results may have given you a sense of powerlessness and hopelessness, so that you are saying, "Yeah, this is all well and good for her, but it won't work for me. Nothing works for me." Allow me to point out that if you are reading and absorbing the material in this book, you are not in the same place you were before. You may look the same, but you know more. One of the things you know is that at least one person who felt as helpless as you do has recovered.

Who can you trust as you avail yourself of the puzzle pieces set before you?

I place greater confidence in people who know and care about me personally, and/or in those who are knowledgeable on the subject about which they speak. This knowledge might be based on education and training, on their experience working in the area, or on their own life experience. Don't be afraid to ask questions about an advisor's background or the rationale for their advice. **In addition, I am more likely to take the advice of a Christian whose life demonstrates that he or she is reasonable and godly.** Thirdly, when I am skeptical about a suggestion, **I look for confirmation**. Does a second trustworthy, mature source support the same idea?

I also measure everything against scripture. If a principle or a practice does not directly contradict God's Word, then it might be worth considering. Jesus said in Luke 9:50, "He that is not against us is for us." Of course, this presumes that you are highly familiar with and grounded in God's Word so that you can make the comparisons. If you are not, I recommend that you get acquainted.

I do not expect to benefit from a resource or from words of counsel if I have not also prayed about the matter at hand. In a multitude of Old Testament verses, God warns His people against looking to chariots, horses, or foreign nations to bring them victory in battle (and against looking to physicians for healing) without looking to Him first. God has used and may still use humans and man-made instruments to accomplish His purposes in war or healing or teaching, but He places a premium on our consulting Him first and looking to Him ultimately for successful results. Therefore, I suggest that you never trust anyone or anything *instead of* God or without first asking if this is how His will is to be done. If you are walking close to God and He does not give you a distinct "red light," then perhaps the direction you feel led to go is from Him and you have a green light to proceed.

It's gonna take time.

I wrote the song "It's Gonna Take Time" in 1989, and I have used it, along with "Shifting Tides," to minister to hurting clients and workshop participants. May you find the words encouraging and not discouraging:

It's Gonna Take Time

Vs. 1:
There was a time when my world collapsed and
  depression owned me.
I was withdrawn and even in a crowd I still felt lonely.
I wasn't myself, and my oldest friends just wouldn't
  have known me.
I really needed to be revived, restored, and remade.

Chorus:
And the Lord said to me, "I know you don't like
  feeling this way.
I know you're wond'ring how you're gonna make it
  through another day.
I know you're wond'ring why I don't just touch you
  and make you feel fine.
Well, **we've got a lot of work to do on you, and it's
gonna take time."**

Vs. 2:
This was the time when I had a lot of growing up to
  do.
**And the Lord said, "I wanna see a change in ways
and in attitude.**
You need to be transformed by having your mind
  renewed." *
I knew I needed to be revived, restored, and remade.

Chorus again:

150

Vs. 3:

**The Master Potter went to work on me with His
loving hands.**
**I've been through the fire, and ready for use this
vessel stands.**
**And though I know that He isn't finished with me
yet,**
**Still I can say, "I've been revived, restored, and
remade."**

New Chorus:
And the Lord said to me, "You're gonna feel a lot
better this way."
Well, He was right, and now there aren't hours enough
each day
To do all the things He's given me the power and joy
to do.
I've got so much to thank Him for that it's gonna take
time!

Coda: And I'm so glad I have eternity, 'cause it's
gonna take time.

*Romans 12:2   © 1989 Susan F. Tackett

If time drags for you, as it once did for me, then you can
appreciate how far I had come when I could write the words of
the Coda and mean them.

151

Chapter 19

Is It Worth It?

The day arrived when I was able to consider life outside the hospital with something other than anxiety. I bought the December issue of a couple of magazines in the hospital gift shop (using Aunt Mildred's money), and browsing through them, I began to get into the Christmas spirit. I actually felt a little excitement and anticipation. This was a miracle as far as I was concerned.

I allowed myself to think about going home for good. I was not positive that I had a guaranteed roof over my head, but no threats had been uttered since the Saturday before I entered the hospital, so I dared to assume that I could return home.

One of the patients in our unit, Patsy, was not highly motivated in recovery, because her husband had told her that when she was discharged, he was going to divorce her. I did not have to face this, but I did wonder what I had ahead of me. I didn't know then that John had considered divorce while I was in St. Mark's. Perhaps this was one occasion when ignorance was bliss, or at least advantageous.

Am I worth it?

One of the things I had been wrestling with during my stay was my value as a human being. A number of things had combined to make it difficult for me to look people in the eye. **So in addition to questioning if the work of recovery was worth it, I sometimes wondered if I was worth it. I made progress in this area thanks to my searching of the scriptures.**

Several months prior to entering the hospital I had set a goal of reading the entire Bible. I was not reading straight through but in a sequence that was meaningful to me, and I was taking my time; I did not want to rush through it briskly just so I could say I had read it all.

When I entered St. Mark's I still had about six books to go, mostly in the New Testament, and I completed the reading during my time there. The gospel of John and the book of Revelation (also written by John) were among the books I wanted to finish. I don't remember now which other books I read, because I also searched through the Bible as a whole during that time, finding many good things.

My discoveries gave me a foundation for healthy self-esteem.

Actually, the discovery did not lie in the verses themselves but in my ability to trust them. I did not particularly need to find a great number of passages that reassured me of my worth. What I needed was to be able to have confidence in the ones I had already found.

John 3:16 told me that God loved me; 1 Peter 5:7 told me I could cast all my "anxiety" upon God because He cares for me. The gospel of John, especially in chapters fourteen through seventeen where Jesus explains things to his disciples during the Last Supper, was replete with talk of love. "He who loves me will be loved by my Father, and I too will love him and show myself to him" (14:21b). Jesus even prayed for all of us who would believe in him.

If Jesus loved me enough to die for me, to send me a Counselor, and to intercede for me, then I must have some worth. This worth did not have anything to do with my successes or failures, but simply with who I am as a creation of God and as His child.

Nor did my worth have anything to do with my feelings. By now I was prepared to accept that if the Bible said something was so, then it was so. If God valued me enough to redeem me, then I was valuable whether I felt so or not. I was able to trust that God loved and accepted me NO MATTER WHAT. If God is love and is also unchanging, then His love for me establishes my value or worth in an unequivocal way.

To sum it up: I am not valuable because a person or philosophy says so (a good thing, since people are fickle and philosophies come and go); nor because I wish to be so; nor because I feel so; nor because I earn the right to be so. I am valuable because God confers the value. He loves us. Period.

I also took to heart Jesus's words in John 10:28-29 that no one can snatch us out of his or the Father's hands. These were reassuring words, building in a security which nothing on the inside or outside of St. Mark's could undermine.

Have you ever wondered why the "paralytic's" friends (Lk. 5) took the initiative to take him to Jesus, other than the obvious reason that he could not walk there himself? There is no record of his even asking for help; his friends simply intervened. Is it possible that the man didn't feel that he was worth the trouble? I had felt that way for a while. Now I was beginning to grasp that, even when I had doubted my own worth, I was no less valuable to God. I could identify with the man in the story. My depression and anxiety had paralyzed me in some ways. God used a number of people to get me the help I needed, and He met me Himself. Soon I would be ready to take up my mat and go home.

Do not doubt if you are worth it - worth the time, trouble, and expense of getting help. Do not doubt God's love for you. And do not doubt that God has a purpose for you.

Believers are meant to be overcomers.

A second way in which scripture helped me was in building my confidence as an overcomer. I gained a **new understanding of my identity in Christ and the righteousness, value, and power or strength this confers.** John liked to write about this. **Jesus was and is an overcomer - "I have overcome the world" (Jn. 16:33) - and we can be, too, because of our identity in him and his spirit within us.**

I had said that I wanted peace that would overcome all circumstances; I wanted to walk above the waves and not be sucked down emotionally. I was learning to do this by seeking for peace in the proper place and developing a resistance to other influences. Now I was realizing that overcoming meant even more than this: Jesus gave us the authority to tread over all the power of our spiritual enemy (Lk. 10:19), and he assured us that we would do greater things than he did (Jn. 14:12).

Revelation promises magnificent rewards to overcomers. Reading Revelation was a stirring experience for me. Having accepted the lack of proof in spiritual matters, I was able to take Revelation entirely on faith. As Paul Harvey would say, **I knew "the rest of the story," and I found it invigorating.** Whatever difficulties my life might still hold for me, they would be temporary. I knew what lay on the other side.

Gary Smalley has said that the reason the disciples panicked when their boat was tossed about on the Sea of Galilee was that they had overlooked the assurance, the implied certainty, in Jesus's words about crossing "to the other side" (Mt. 8:18). If we are guaranteed a safe arrival, why worry about the hardships on the journey?

I had never heard of Gary Smalley at that time, but sitting on my hospital bed, reading the last book of the Bible, **I could see**

155

that down the line I am guaranteed a safe arrival in heaven and a glorious eternity, so whatever lay between the present and that destination did not seem to matter so much. Jesus, "for the joy set before him endured the cross, scorning its shame, and sat down at the right hand of the throne of God" (Heb. 12: 2b). For the joy ahead of me, I could face whatever work or pain or hardships might precede it.

God's promise to me that many people would benefit from my experience began to seem less ludicrous. After all, if God was able to see the events described in Revelation, then He could surely see my future. Even more than that - **if He could orchestrate the grand scenarios of Revelation, He could certainly manage my life!**

An undefeated spirit.

In keeping with my earlier promise to God to enjoy every blessing and be thankful, I also resolved to be less of a whiner. I wanted to be a person of great faith (and a good attitude). If CTU could have a motto, then I could, too, and I selected the words "undefeated spirit" to describe the new person I believed I was becoming. I resolved to let nothing get me down in my spirit. By the way, Smalley says that murmurers have "dinky faith." I did not, and do not now, want to settle for dinky faith.

Encouraging words.

I continued to receive cards and letters of encouragement. One of these was from Daddy. I share parts of it here in the hope that his words will speak to you, too:

Dear Susan,

I hope this reaches you by Wednesday, so you will have mail before Thanksgiving..... Lots of things to be

156

thankful for - the love and support of families whether in a time of special need or not; the care we can receive from others who have prepared themselves to help; maybe most of all the strength that God gives us to pull ourselves through times when we've run to the end of our own limits and feel too far gone to feel we can make it. I don't believe that God gives us troubles to strengthen us - we generate most of them ourselves - but **He gives us the opportunity to learn and grow from them**, even if it does seem as if the price is sometimes awfully high.

My experience has been that there is a comfort from being able to tell yourself, "I've coped with that kind of problem before and I won!" My prayers are with you and I'm as near as your telephone....

Love,
Dad

I did have mixed feelings about going home, as you can discern from one of my written assignments: "We need a new beginning together. I feel a little distant from John and yet I know he loves me. I hope that we will be two stronger individuals and will have a healthier marriage. I feel a little afraid." **Notice the word "little" appears twice. I was no longer feeling *great* distance or *overwhelming* fear, a dramatic change for me.**

Two letters that I received encouraged me on the matter of going home. The first was from Rosemary and was dated Sunday, November 25. She said she believed that if I would depend on John less for help and constant companionship, he and I would both find this rewarding. She went on to say,

You sound so good on the phone. You are taking the responsibility for yourself and seem pleased with it. You think the medicine is helping, you think the

157

therapy is good, you like Dr. Mason, and you are willing to stay until you feel ready to go home, and I think this is super. I just feel **you are going to be a stronger and happier person**.... I feel there is no love lost between you and John. A good, uninterrupted, honest talk about what both of you want out of life and maybe from one another will surely make things "right" again. Maybe there are changes that need to be made – do you think?....

The second encouraging letter was from an older woman in our congregation who was a good friend to all five of us. Among other things, she wrote,

Enjoyed your note so much and we all are glad to know that you are improving..... You have three super-active boys, and take advice from one that loves you, don't come home until you feel that you can cope with them. We sure don't want you to undo all the progress that you are making. Just live each day as it comes along and know that with each day you are getting stronger and stronger. **God is your strength and He will see you through this if you continue to pray and trust** in your loving God.

I wish I could have known then what Nathan shared with me recently. Nathan is the only one of my sons who remembers much about November and December of 1984. He remembers my being gone only "a short while" and that his grandparents and Aunt Sarah helped out. He does not remember feeling worried or embarrassed or abandoned. **Nathan says, "If everyone's intention was to keep life normal for us, it worked." This suggests two things: the efforts of John, his parents, my sister, and our Christian friends made a positive difference for our sons; and kids are resilient - life goes on.** Your fears that your condition is forever ruining your child's life may be exaggerated.

Were my recovery efforts worth it?

I could not yet know how things would go when I returned home, but I could see that God and I together were making a difference in my own life. I was definitely feeling and functioning better. I had a family waiting for me who needed me, so long as I could be more adult than child, and an able God to go with me.

I loved my family dearly, and now, when I thought of them, I experienced feelings of affection without the guilt. In spite of some unresolved issues with John, I was eager to move forward with him. I could look at the portraits of my sons and smile as I anticipated being with them again: Nathan with his love of books, music, and adventure; Seth, sensitive but daring, who liked anything with wheels and an engine; and Joseph, good-natured and easy-to-please. **Now that I could believe I was not on a permanent downward course, I could afford to look forward, and I did so with hope. I actually FELT hopeful!** The positive changes and signs of life gave my momentum a real boost. Yes, this was worth it.

Know who you are and whose you are.

I want to close this chapter with a piece from Robert McGee's *Search for Significance*. I hope it will edify and encourage you.

My Identity in Christ

Because of Christ's redemption,
I am a new creation of infinite worth.
I am deeply loved,
I am completely forgiven,
I am fully pleasing,
I am totally accepted by God.

I am absolutely complete in Christ.
When my performance
reflects my new identity in Christ,
that reflection is dynamically unique.
There has never been another person like me
in the history of mankind,
nor will there ever be.
God has made me an original,
one of a kind, really somebody!

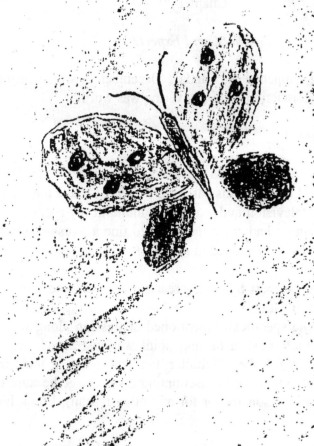

MY PERSONAL SYMBOL OF CHANGE....

(expressive therapy - fourth or fifth week;
done in bright colors)

Chapter 20

What Can I Expect?

Something happened on Sunday, December 2, which further increased my conviction that persevering was worth it.

A turning point.

On Sunday mornings mass was held in the chapel, but being a Protestant, I did not go. This particular Sunday I found the "Hour of Power" on television and watched it alone in my room. This was the only time I had made the effort to find a worship service on TV God must have moved in my heart.

I listened as Robert Schuller preached a message on turning points. He said that no matter what kind of suffering we were in the midst of (he specifically mentioned depression along with a couple of other things), a turning point was just ahead. I had never been a big Robert Schuller fan, but today I took the message to heart. Instead of discounting his message because he didn't know me personally (or for any other reason), I took him seriously.

About four o'clock that same afternoon, I suddenly KNEW that the worst was behind me - that I had bottomed out and started back up. The realization was so dramatic that I looked at the clock to mark this moment in time. I would never again be as bad off as I had been, and from this moment on I could be assured of being on the way up. Did I hear an audible voice? No, but I was as certain of the message as if I had. I believed I would get well. The message must have been from God, because I have NEVER again been at the bottom of the pit.

The next weekend I began planning for Christmas. Somehow we all knew - staff, patients, and myself - that my discharge was fast approaching. I started a to-do list. I was excited and felt like I had the pep to pull off the tasks I was including in it. I was so pleased that I would have enough time before Christmas to shop and decorate the house and a tree. Joseph's second birthday was December 6, and the family postponed celebrating until I could be home to join in.

A moment of near-ecstasy occurred one day in expressive therapy. We had rolls of butcher paper or newsprint, and we were to lie down on a big sheet of it while someone else drew around us. I think we were then supposed to discuss our self-concepts or self-esteem, but we never got that far. Ann and I, good buddies by this time, teamed up. I sat on the floor, drawing around her with a marker and my hand slipped. When she stood up, the silhouette looked as if she had an extra appendage protruding from her right side. We both cracked up at the grotesqueness of it, and I literally rolled on the floor with laughter. What a release! I laughed till I cried. It felt wonderful to let go so completely, and without Xanax!

The other marvel is that the comedy was produced at my expense, because of my mistake. The error could not be erased or covered up, so we left it alone. My ability to laugh at myself was a good sign. It meant I was not as self-conscious and not taking myself so seriously. I didn't feel any compulsion to explain my mistake to the rest of the group. I just enjoyed it. In general I was getting a better perspective on myself in the context of other people. I did not have to be perfect. Ann did not make fun of me or get upset; she simply laughed with me. I still chuckle as I write about this. Perhaps some folks need to take themselves more seriously, but I had needed to lighten up.

The word "fun" was re-entering my vocabulary. One morning Dana brought a little painted creature back from ceramics class and I thought, "Why didn't I do ceramics?" Her creation was cute, and I regretted that I had missed the opportunity to have such fun.

Acceptance of reality.

In some areas of my life, I was taking first steps, but in one area, I made huge strides before I ever left the hospital. I can best describe this as acceptance. Now that I did not feel anxious about every little thing, I could sit back and look at life more objectively. I could see that life was inevitably going to involve discomfort, pain, sacrifice, suffering, and risk. Furthermore, I could accept this and I felt ready to face it.

Life is not like a game of Sorry, where you can physically escape to a Safety Zone - removed from circulation so that nothing can touch you. Until we reach heaven, there will be unpleasantness and worse. In fact, I could see that **if I were to make my choices and live my life with safety as my ultimate goal, risks would still be involved.** Staying home might prevent automobile accidents, but I would miss interesting travel experiences and could still die in a house fire; withdrawing from certain social situations might prevent hurt or humiliation but would risk loneliness and reduce opportunities for Christian witnessing. Playing it safe would risk the loss of my mental health and my family. Now that life looked good again, I wanted to LIVE.

Scott Peck writes of acceptance in the opening lines of *The Road Less Traveled*: "Life is difficult. This is a great truth, one of the greatest truths.... Once we truly know that life is difficult - once we truly understand and accept it - then life is no longer difficult. Because once it is accepted, the fact that life is difficult no longer matters."

As long as we are not accepting the difficulties of life, we are resisting or fighting life. Futile combat wastes our energy and drains our concentration away from more worthwhile matters. I like the way Gary Smalley describes this struggle. He says we "stiffarm reality." I had been doing that with all my

164

complaints about how I shouldn't feel this way and people shouldn't be doing this and saying that. Also, my excessive worrying had really been an expression of a belief that life shouldn't be this way! As if, at some point, life was going to smooth out and deliver everything I wanted - as if life *should* do this. **Once I accepted the realities that life is hard AND that God would sustain me through it all, it was as if I had pulled anchor and could sail.**

Until Revelation's events have all transpired, this world is going to remain the way it is or worse, **so let's not waste our efforts fighting what we cannot change.** Remember the Serenity Prayer. Let's discriminate, with God's help, between those things we can control or change and those we cannot. We can prevent or ease some hardship, and we can certainly minister to those who are suffering through various tribulations, but we are not going to experience a totally easy and pain-free existence on this planet.

I began to see that accepting hardship and risks was not only necessary, but was actually desirable in God's eyes. In the parable of the talents in the gospel of Matthew, the fearful servant who hid his talent was regarded as "wicked" and "lazy." The ones who were able to return more to the master than they were given in the first place were regarded as "good and faithful." Their efforts had involved risks without guarantees, and the master found their faithfulness worthy of reward. By the way, we don't know if they *felt* fearful; what we know is that **they did the right thing whether or not they felt afraid.**

This is war!

Meanwhile, where IS the battle? The real warfare for us as Christians is against Satan. Satan is out to "steal, kill, and destroy" (Jn. 10:10), especially hearts, minds, families, and testimonies. We are on the winning side; let's live like it. Every time we demonstrate love to another human being, introduce someone to Jesus, teach the truth, exhibit the fruit of the Spirit, help another Christian discover their full identity in Christ, discern evil at work and put a stop to it, or praise God, we are furthering God's kingdom and taking territory from the enemy. Satan would have liked to make me an ineffective witness, doubting God and too fearful to step out in faith and love. He almost succeeded. But God's love pulled me back from the edge and empowered me to live boldly.

Steven Biko courageously and peacefully pushed forward the battle against apartheid in South Africa in the 1970's. He was banished to a specific location but occasionally slipped out in order to live a normal life and encourage others in the struggle for freedom. In one scene in *Cry Freedom* he said this: "Yes, of course I take risks - all the time. But that is only unusual if you think we're a land at peace. You see, **in a war, people take great risks as a part of life. Well....we're at war.**"

I like this, because it describes our status as Christians. We are engaged in spiritual warfare, as Paul describes in Ephesians 6. Sometimes we push forward; sometimes we simply stand firm. This mean that we not only face the same earthly risks everyone else faces, but additional ones. We risk being persecuted for our faith. **Even those of us who don't risk life and limb in the foreign mission field still risk being disappointed, humiliated, maligned, or unpopular.**

At the very least, if we live for Christ at all, we risk the inconvenience of the spiritual disciplines and of interruptions in our schedules by people who need us. If I am not willing to sacrifice some of my personal time, how am I going to help a suicidal person? If I am not willing to risk appearing foolish, how am I going to help the person who says he thinks something evil has a grip on him? If I am not willing to risk making a mistake, how am I going to teach a seminar?

If I believe that I must be liked and approved of by every individual, how am I going to set proper limits with people? If I am overly afraid of hurting or offending someone, how am I going to offer tough love to them when they need it? If I am afraid of getting too close to someone, or fear that I will let them down, how am I going to offer the soft love and compassion they need? **If I am not willing to take risks and get out of my comfort zone, how am I going to be Christlike? Knowing what lay ahead of him, Jesus still set his face toward Jerusalem!** (Lk. 9:51)

So how do we do this? How do we conduct ourselves in this battle? We put on and keep on our armor (apply Ephesians 6), we train ourselves in godliness (study and apply the rest of God's Word), and we obediently heed the voice of our Commanding Officer (consult God in prayer). Remember that nothing can separate you from "the love of God that is in Christ Jesus" (Rom. 8:39) and that in all things that life and Satan can throw at you, "we are more than conquerors" (Rom. 8:37).

This isn't heaven, but it can be pretty good anyway!

Having described the negative aspects of life, let me say this: when Jesus promised us trouble in this world (Jn. 16:33), he also promised us his peace and his joy (15:11). He said that he came to give us abundant life (Jn. 10:10, *KJV*), so he obviously did not expect us to be miserable and mournful all the time.

In *When God Whispers Your Name,* Max Lucado makes two points that are helpful. One is that **we should not expect earth to deliver what only heaven can deliver, and we will find greater peace when we accept this. We will inevitably be dissatisfied if we expect life to be perfect in an imperfect, fallen world. His second point is that, in spite of the above, life on earth does afford us many blessings and opportunities.**

167

Lucado says that as Christians we should be enjoying life, and he suggests that one of the reasons Jesus went to weddings was simply that he enjoyed them. I like this! Being serious about being a Christian does not mean that you cannot enjoy life.

In the Serenity Prayer, Reinhold Niebuhr includes both of these phrases: "enjoying one moment at a time" and "taking this sinful world as it is....not as I would have it." We can enjoy the blessings of this life while also accepting that there will be messes. Please don't misunderstand me; **I am not promoting complacency, but acceptance**. Complacency causes us to remain inactive even when we COULD make a difference.

In the movie and book *Charlotte's Web*, whose main characters are barnyard animals, a baby gosling steps out of the nest for the first time and looks around.

"It's big out here," he says.

The mama goose responds, **"It is big and it is frightening at times, but on the whole the world is a wonderful place."**

Have you ever seen the movie *Old Yeller*? The story takes place in 1860's Texas. Some of the best lines ever uttered about acceptance are spoken towards the end. Travis and a friend have just buried Travis's beloved Old Yeller.

Papa Jim comes upon the scene. "One of the roughest things I ever heard tell of...The thing to do now is try and forget it, and go on being a man," Papa says.

Travis asks, "How do you forget something like that?"

His father replies,

"I guess I don't quite mean that. That's not a thing you can forget. Maybe not even a thing you want to forget. What I'm trying to say is, **life is like that sometimes. Now and then, for no good reason a man can figure out, life will just haul off and knock him flat - slam him agin' the ground so hard it seems like all his insides is busted. It's not all like that. A lot of it's mighty fine. You can't afford to waste the good part frettin' about the bad.** That makes it all bad..... Sure, I know. Saying it's one thing and feelin' it's another. But I'll tell you a trick that's sometimes a big help. **When you start looking around for something good to take the place of the bad, as a general rule you can find it.**"

The value of adversity.

Barbara Johnson says, "Experience is what you get when you didn't get what you wanted." I had never wanted to be depressed, anxious, or hospitalized, but I did gain experience, and a learning one at that. As I mentioned in Chapter 17, **I have acquired a whole new perspective on suffering, a glimpse of which I caught as I was preparing to leave St. Mark's.**

The writer of Hebrews describes hardship as training in God's holiness that will produce **"a harvest of righteousness and peace** for those who have been trained by it" (12: 11). And Paul wrote in Romans 8:28 that "in all things God works for the good of those who love him, who have been called according to his purpose." **God has definitely used my illness and hospitalization to bring about good.**

First of all, God used my experience to benefit others right away. I have a note from our church organist in which she encouraged me ("with a lot of determination and the prayers of your friends, wonders have been accomplished"), and then she went on to say, "so much love has been shown that I think it has 'rubbed off' on the whole church." Our church family was generous and helpful with John and the boys, and they prayed steadfastly for all of us. I think they also grew in compassion during this time, and in their appreciation for this "new" kind of suffering that their pastor's wife was experiencing.

Secondly, most of the good things that God has done in or through me in my adult life can be traced back to St. Mark's. I would leave the hospital not just feeling better and thinking straighter, but with strength, understanding, compassion, and a confidence in God which I had not had before. Fortitude, stamina, and greater resolve developed out of this experience and have served me well. If suffering makes you either "bitter or better," as Smalley suggests, then I am so grateful that I let God take me the "better" route.

Philip Gulley's story, "Growing Roots," is appropriate here. He writes about Dr. Gibbs, a neighbor who planted trees years ago and then hardly ever watered them, because he believed that watering plants would spoil them, producing successively weaker generations of "weenie trees." Dr. Gibbs believed that if trees were not watered frequently, they would have to put down deeper roots in search of moisture.

Dr. Gibbs also beat each oak "with a rolled up newspaper....to get the tree's attention." Twenty-five years later those robust trees "wake up in the morning and beat their chests and drink their coffee black," while Gulley's own "sissy trees" tremble at the least sign of a wind.

Gulley comments that **adversity and deprivation actually seem to have benefited the doctor's trees.** Cold winds are inevitable, and the deep roots that are put down during hard times will hold a tree steady and firm. **Gulley says we should be praying not for ease but for deep roots.** My experience in the pit did strengthen me for the long haul. I would leave St. Mark's with my roots extending deeper than ever before.

Perhaps this is the kind of thing James had in mind when he wrote, "Consider it pure joy, my brothers, whenever you face trials of many kinds, because you know that **the testing of your faith develops perseverance.** Perseverance must finish its work so that you may be mature and complete, not lacking anything" (1:2-3). Paul wrote, "...we also rejoice in our sufferings, because we know that suffering produces perseverance; perseverance, character; and character, hope (Rom. 5: 3-4).

Barbara Johnson says that her life took a dramatic turn for the better when she learned to say, "Whatever, Lord," instead of "Why me?" So now, when hard times come my way, I try to maintain a sense of humor and an openness to whatever God wants to teach me. During a period of anguishing legal proceedings in my life, I was able to say, "Okay, God, what are we learning this time?"

I cannot say that I enjoy suffering. As Hebrews says, "No discipline seems pleasant at the time, but painful" (12:11), but I can look beyond the experience to becoming more Christlike through it and even farther to an eternity with Christ himself. For inspiring and moving reading on the value of adversity, read Melody Beattie's *The Lessons of Love.*

Breaking free!

The day before I was to be discharged from St. Mark's, I was asked to complete a Progress Note on myself. I was to fill this out *as if I were the doctor* observing me. For some reason I did not refer to my original goal sheet. Here is what I wrote:

THERAPIST EVALUATION/OBSERVATIONS
OF PATIENT: Stronger in terms of physical energy,

171

voice tone, and confidence in self. Friendlier, smiling more, more limber physically (relaxed and loose). Does not look or sound as depressed though nervous and shaky.

PATIENT'S PROGRESS TOWARD GOAL/GOALS :
1. eat 3 good meals a day   Has accomplished all
2. sleep soundly till reasonable hour   of these; still
3. no panic attacks   somewhat nervous or
4. more energy   anxious off and on

Looks better and sounds better. Was obsessed with physical complaints - a worrier, but now seems to be taking things in stride better. Has accomplished: new resolutions for how to proceed; has worked at understanding herself and her relationships by opening up & by listening to others; is taking satisfactory dosage of medication; has self (body & health) in better perspective.

Dana gave me an "I'm-going-to-miss-you" card. Patsy put her arm around me one day as we were leaving group and said, "What are we going to do around with here without you. You've been our angel." The affection and support felt great.

Patsy also wrote me a short letter, which I saved:

Dear Susan,

I am sorry we couldn't do anything special with you on your last day here, but I do want to let you know how comforting your support and concern have been to me. So often I don't share my inner feelings; please know that they are there. I'm saddened you're leaving because I find it a loss; on the other hand I am very happy for you and I am convinced you'll be able to handle the difficult situation at home quite well. Know that you'll be in my prayers and in my thoughts. God love you and keep you!

Lots of love,
Patsy

172

On December 12, I told everyone "good-bye" and left the fifth floor behind me. I've never been back.

I felt exhilaration mixed with a little apprehension as John and I carried my bags to the car. As I stepped into the sunlight and brisk air, I felt like I was being born all over again. I caught my breath.

I thought of my butterfly drawing and imagined myself breaking out of a cocoon. Tentative but excited, I was ready to fly!

He redeems my life

from the pit

and crowns me

with love and compassion.

Psalm 103:4

PART THREE:

LIVING AS AN OVERCOMER

...those who hope in the Lord
will renew their strength.
They will soar on wings like eagles;
they will run and not grow weary,
they will walk and not faint.

Isaiah 40:31

The Sovereign Lord is my strength;
he makes my feet like the feet of a deer,
he enables me to go on the heights.

Habakkuk 3:19

Chapter 21

Alive Again!

I was overjoyed to be home again. We all fell into the most smooth and normal routine we had experienced in a year or two. The holidays were thoroughly enjoyable, and my enthusiasm and energy never sagged.

I had expected some aftershock in the boys' behavior or my relationships with them, but we resumed as if I had never been gone. The one exception was that, for a few weeks, Joseph stuck more closely than usual to my side. He wanted to snuggle and especially to "wock and wead."

Collecting my thoughts.

Rosemary sent me a beautiful 1985 journal which I began using on New Year's, recording goals and some of the lessons I'd learned in 1984. My goals included such areas as self-care, prayer and Bible study, housekeeping and organizing, my relationships with John and the boys, specific things I wanted each son to learn or master that year, and ministry to others outside the family. Now that I no longer took life for granted, I wanted to make each day count!

This writing established a pattern which I continued daily for several months and less frequently for several years. Putting my thoughts on paper helped to clear my head and give me checkpoints for progress. As I read through my journal now, I see that most of what I did that year was in keeping with my goals. **I would again encourage you to set some objectives for yourself and purposefully set about reaching them (without being a slave to them).**

I concluded my first-of-the-year thoughts with this:

> This is an official new beginning for me as a person and
> with my family, friends, and community. I am excited
> and hopeful about this second chance at Life. Looking
> back (or too far ahead) makes me sad or fearful, so I will
> try to take one day at a time. My anxious and depressed
> moments are rare now and I am more easily distracted
> from them. My three weeks at home have gone beautifully!

My journal entries contain references to making snow ice
cream, Nathan's Pinewood Derby, Seth's learning to read simple
books to Joseph, and Joseph's learning to climb out of the crib,
and, when summer rolled around, to tee-ball, fishing, outdoor
barbecues, a trip to the zoo, and church camp. I made numerous
notes throughout these months regarding a building program at
church, an undertaking about which John was both enthused and
stressed. He capably and successfully led the church through this
time, and I was proud of him.

What about the marriage?

John seemed appreciative of my efforts to carry my share of
the responsibilities. He trusted me more, especially to manage
satisfactorily when he was gone over night, and shared more of
his own feelings with me than in a long time. We had a new
respect for each other's individuality and were less inclined to
take each other for granted. I wrote, "Feel very close sometimes,
but the strain of the last few months shows itself in coolness or
impatience."

One of our bonding moments was when John presented me
with a small but meaningful gift, a delicate candleholder with a
pink candle in it. I don't remember exactly what he said, but it
was something romantic and contained a hint of new beginnings;

I was overcome by warm, fuzzy feelings. At times like this we felt like newlyweds enjoying a fresh start.

January did bring some painful remarks my way, as I mentioned earlier. It hurt me to think that both John and his mother felt (at least at times) that I didn't deserve a second chance and was being given one only because John condescended. I found myself wondering if they would pass judgment so harshly on everyone who had been depressed and anxious; if they wanted me to feel guilty or indebted forever; and whether he had meant "in sickness or in health." Unfortunately such thoughts fueled dissatisfaction rather than peace.

I tried to be gracious enough to simply pick up where we were without dwelling on the past or on these remarks. I told myself that John and his family simply wanted me to appreciate that he had been through quite an ordeal himself and they simply overstated their case. Because I had needed John to be forbearing with me, I tried not to be begrudging towards him.

Still an undercurrent of mutual, unresolved anger persisted and reared its head from time to time. John apparently still held my illness (which he would not accept as illness) against me. If he had fully understood my experience and how hard I had fought to overcome it, there would have been no room in his heart for condemning thoughts.

By the same token, if I had known the full extent of my harsh words and irritability in previous months, I might have understood his assertion that I was just plain mean. He also told me on one occasion that he was tired of feeling sorry for me and having me run his life. I believe he was understandably tired of arranging his life around my needs and dependence on him. While I was doing everything I could to change that pattern, and even vowed to be more like a wife and less like a daughter to him, he may have needed

me to voice a greater acceptance of his frustration. **Neither of us did enough listening, active empathizing, or forgiving.**

If you are married and your spouse has difficulty accepting you, try understanding his point of view first. Perhaps he needs empathy and appreciation as much as you do, in which case, he may need you to give him a chance to talk about how your illness has affected him, and he definitely needs to have you express some gratitude and carry as much of the load as you are able. Allow time for his reservations to be replaced with trust, as you improve.

John and I would pay a high price for our resentments. Don't make the same mistake. If you and your spouse can talk things out in an empathizing, resolving way, do so. But if not, simply acknowledge that neither of you can truly know what it was like to be in the other's shoes during this time and let that be enough. Either way, forgive each other. This situation calls for closure.

Ups and downs.

I cannot say that I had no more emotional problems, but I can say that they were manageable. My mood (which I now realized had been depressed) was consistently brighter, but in January of 1985 I began to experience brief spells of anxiety symptoms along with a more constant free-floating anxiety. I did not like these inexplicable feelings, but I was happy and functioning well in spite of them. **The objective evidence said that I was well on the road to recovery**, and Dr. Mason and Jenny (whom we continued to see together) were pleased with my progress.

Therefore my approach to the nuisance of uneasiness was primarily to ignore it and focus on living well. I did talk to Dr. Mason about it, and he increased the Elavil, adding that I should take a Xanax as needed. I still took a Xanax only rarely, but was thankful for it then. I don't regret that I used Xanax so sparingly, but taking it more often would not have been harmful.

I found ways to cope with Elavil's side effects. My mouth and intestines continued to be dry. A stool softener worked effectively, this time without causing diarrhea or anxiety. Beverages and mints accompanied me everywhere. My morning blood pressure was still low enough to make me feel weak and light-headed, but I went about my activities matter-of-factly, knowing that I would feel better as the morning passed.

A re-awakening.

I did feel like I was coming alive again. I felt a wide range of positive emotions which outweighed the negative ones. My body seemed to be re-awakening, especially my senses and my ability to move freely. Colors seemed brighter, food tasted better, music involved me more, I enjoyed sex and sexual touch again, and, as I stretched my arms and legs one morning before getting out of bed, I realized I had not done so in many months. I cannot explain how anxiety can literally bind up the muscles, but it can.

I clearly remember a special moment with Joseph. I had gone to the master bedroom to put away some laundry. Joseph followed me and climbed up on the bed. He began jumping up and down, laughing and having a grand time, so I stood by the side of the bed and held his hands to keep him from falling. As we laughed and held hands, I suddenly noticed the feel of his chubby little hands in mine. I can't describe what I felt, but it was as if I were rediscovering my sense of touch, as if my hands had been "asleep" and were returning to normal. The pleasure of being with Joseph and sharing his good time were also in that precious touch.

Lessons learned.

On January 8, I took plain paper and typed up some thoughts that were too detailed to cram onto a single journal page. I kept trying to solidify my gains and ensure that I would not lose any ground. Writing these lessons helped me do this. The excerpt below contains what I believed I had learned in recent months:

That those things in the world which give the greatest warmth and hope and sense of usefulness are kind words, an attempt on someone's part to empathize and under-stand, words that compliment or encourage, and hugs.

Not to take health, or a new day or the love or help of another person for granted. All are gifts that can be taken away from us.

That music, books, possessions, nature, people, opportunities, and responsibilities—those same things which, to the depressed person hold no meaning or enjoyment—provide happiness, purpose, and hope to the person who is emotionally healthy and at peace with himself and who feels loved by God and by at least one other human being.

That it is important to be good enough to other people that you feel needed by them and that, if you were gone, no one else could exactly fill your shoes.

That being accepted, loved, encouraged, needed and supported by others is only one part of Life—accepting, loving, encouraging, needing, and supporting others is as important.

That before you can build healthy relationships with others, you must first trust God and take a close look at yourself to know who you are and which parts of yourself to keep and which to discard. But once you have done this, get your mind off yourself; you will only enjoy life and find it meaningful as you pour out your new-found self, loving others in the ways they need to be loved.

I once thought that to feel one's self as indispensable to anyone or any situation was to have too much pride in self.

I was wrong. To love, help, and be involved so little
as to not be missed when gone is not really living.

A devotional.

On January 28, 1985, I wrote a devotional of sorts, which I
recently found folded and stuck between pages of my journal. It
strikes me as both poetic and corny, but it captures what I was
feeling as I left my darkest days behind me. Here it is in its
entirety, though I never fully developed some of the ideas:

> At different times during my hospital stay and in my
> remembrance of it, I have felt myself to be many dif-
> ferent things. I imagined myself as an unborn infant,
> growing and developing in darkness, moving toward
> the time when I would be strong and healthy enough to
> take up existence in the real world. I imagined myself
> as a bulb in the ground, waiting to become a flower, or
> as a seed waiting to become a tree. I imagined myself
> folded in a cocoon, waiting to become a butterfly. I
> felt like a figure in a dream moving against a back-
> ground of darkness, observing myself and seeming
> only partially real.
>
> I tried to hope that with a willingness on my part,
> some nourishment from others, sustenance from God,
> and the mere passing of time, I would be born into, or
> burst forth into, or open my eyes upon the light of day
> and real life. If a plant germinates during the wrong
> season, or a baby is born before it can digest food and
> breathe, or if a cocoon is broken open by outside forces,
> the result is a terrible struggle and sometimes death.
>
> As I've thought of these images, I have recognized a
> common ingredient – new life after near-death. Some-
> times in order for us, God's creations, to become all that
> we have the potential and that God wants us to be, we
> must first be left alone with Him and our own selves,
> fragile and vulnerable in a lonely darkness, and remain

181

there until God and the passing of time have molded a
courage and a vision in us that were only shadows before.

Like Jacob, who wrestled with the angel and carried
both the handicap and the edifying victory of that
experience, and like Paul, who endured persecution
and a thorn in his flesh but also had the confidence
to persevere and triumph, I carry with me the pain
of certain memories and acknowledgements, but also
the faith that God never did, and never will, desert me.
Through the suffering and the challenge to be born, I
have been made and am being made into a new creation.

While "near-death" may sound like an exaggeration, being
alone in the darkness had felt like death. However, now I could
look back and see that this whole process of being made into
something new had begun during those dark times when it
seemed like life was only something I was waiting for.

**There is life in the seed, the bulb, the cocoon, and the
womb, even if at first it does not appear so. If you are still
waiting, know that in one way or another you are gaining
strength, even though you may not see how this is so. This
time will count for something!**

I consider that our present sufferings are
not worth comparing
with the glory that will be revealed in us.

Romans 8:18

Chapter 22

Are We There Yet?

Without dwelling on matters that would not interest you, I would like to tell you what my life was like in the following years and share some ideas on how to stay on the path to wellness.

I continued to do the things I had begun in St. Mark's: untwist my thinking; accept hardship with grace; be assertive and express feelings appropriately; welcome accountability and be okay with myself so that I didn't feel threatened by correction or challenge; discriminatingly accept ideas and resources as answers to prayer; decentralize; avoid special expectations for myself; not allow feelings to be my foundation for faith, hope, or truth; express gratitude to God and others; devour scripture; trust God; and operate from my victorious position in Christ.

More stepping stones.

Early in 1985, a GROW group was begun locally, and I participated from the first night. In weekly meetings we encouraged each other and held each other accountable for working the program, which was contained in a little blue book and supplemented with readings from the "brown book." The principles and practical tips I learned in GROW were invaluable to me. From constant use they became a part of who I am. The emphases were on assuming responsibility for my own recovery no matter how difficult this might be at times, basing my thoughts and behavior on truth and reality, and keeping feelings in proper perspective.

In addition to the above, many other resources helped tremendously: **regular Bible study;** *The Road Less Traveled;*

Healing for Damaged Emotions; **and** *The New Guide to Rational Living*, among others. Learning and growing had become exciting to me. I eagerly read and listened to inspirational and life-changing materials. Though there were times when I had to re-surrender to God and re-commit to doing my part, the healing and changes were real and rewarding. When I found myself begrudging that life seemed more effortless for other people than for me, I didn't let these thoughts roost.

Besides managing some anxiety and my anger towards John, which would erupt in over-reactions, I also was trying to find a healthy way to approach my household responsibilities. Because I was trying so hard to prove myself and to make each day count, I probably over-did housecleaning and straightening. I remember feeling that I needed to compensate for all I had put everyone through, so I became compulsive and driven in this area. I needed to retain genuine zeal over being able to function again but also relax a little (without becoming lazy or dependent). It took a year or so to reach a healthy middle ground.

Three events in the summer of 1985 are worth noting: John and I made an oral contract for dealing with his concerns over my anger and my concerns over being abandoned. We agreed that for one-year, during which time I would continue to pursue recovery, he would promise to support me through thick and thin, even if I had to go back to the hospital. We would re-evaluate our marriage at the end of one year. What I gained was the reassurance that I would still have my family for at least that long. What John gained was an "out" if he felt after a year that he could not live with me any longer.

The second event was that both Nathan and Seth invited Jesus into their hearts at church camp that summer, a real morale-booster for all of us. And, thirdly, I undertook to examine both my original family system and my belief system. I evaluated the traits and relationship styles of family members to see which of these I wanted to exhibit (or avoid) and then my own basic beliefs to see which of these were sound and which were not. These processes helped to round out a healthier life for me.

I doubt it would be of any help to you for me to share more about my family, though you might want to scrutinize your own. You do stand to gain by my sharing about faulty beliefs. **Some of the beliefs which I** *dropped* **in favor of more truthful ones were: It is a dire necessity that I be loved and approved of, especially by everyone I consider significant; I should be thoroughly competent, adequate, and achieving in all possible respects; if things do not go the way I want them to, that would be catastrophic or awful; it is easier to avoid responsibilities and difficulties than to face them** (Ellis and Harper, 1975). Months before, I had begun grasping that these were not healthy ideas. As I read more about them, I became even more determined to tone down the extremes in my thinking.

The going gets smoother.

As I became more flexible, spontaneous, and self-confident, better able to accommodate Elavil's side-effects, and less rattled by panic attacks (see Appendix A), I became more willing to try new things and new variations on old activities. I became the organist at church and thoroughly enjoyed playing. I became more involved in my sons' outside activities and assumed a leadership role in GROW. I was not inhibited by the pervasive apprehensions I'd had before, so when new opportunities arose, I changed my tune from "Why?" to "Why not?"

In July 1986, John and I reached the end of our contract and willingly chose to keep moving forward together. When August rolled around, **I recorded in my journal a list of fears, anxieties, and compulsions that I had overcome, and the list is LONG. Not only had I overcome them, but I can report that I have had no trouble with them since. Praise God!** (Take

185

storms for instance—I not only don't fear them; I throw open the door so I can enjoy the smell of rain; even tornado warnings don't stir up much anxiety, though I do take necessary precautions.)

In 1987 we moved to a new community and church. I joined more volunteer mental health organizations, offering both leadership and one-on-one help to individuals in emotional trouble.

I did take Elavil for several years. My philosophy was that if I could learn to be healthier in my thoughts, behavior, and relationships, then I would not need the Elavil forever, but I knew these changes would take time. Also, I did not want to stop the medication too soon and experience the discouragement of a relapse. Dr. Mason and I agreed on this approach, so we did not rush. For a while I was on an increased dosage due to the anxiety (Elavil treats this as well as depression), and I held at that level for a year or so. Then periodically, as Dr. Mason and I would agree that I was stronger and more stable, we reduced the dosage. This method worked well for me. I was ready for each adjustment, and the changes were not noticeable in how I felt or functioned. Could I have managed without the medication earlier? Possibly, but I was and am satisfied with the way I proceeded. By the way, you may reach total wellness and be medication-free sooner than I was if you don't have as far to go.

Will I ever feel this bad again?

You may be wondering what you have in store regarding further depression or anxiety. **About half of individuals who experience one episode of depression will have another. Some people use medication in a preventive way to avoid relapse. Relapse will also be less likely if you follow any suggestions in this book that apply to you.** No matter what caused your depression, unlearning certain beliefs, attitudes, and expectations will decrease the frequency and intensity of future episodes. For the best prognosis, develop a healthy lifestyle in every respect.

In spite of much change in me and the huge repertoire of coping and living skills I learned, I still have *tendencies* in a depressive and anxious direction. I can think of two possible explanations for this. The first is that genetics continue to play a part, so the best approach is to do what I would do with any other inherited condition—take care of myself, try to prevent symptoms, and when that is not enough, learn to manage well in spite of them.

A second possibility is that certain personality types (which a person may have from birth) are more predisposed to depression and anxiety. I am a Choleric Melancholy (see Florence Littauer's materials), and we just naturally take things too seriously. Other personality types are predisposed to different problems. If you find, as Paul did, that you continually do what you "do not want to do" (Rom. 7:19), perhaps your natural personality has run amuck. Even here, you and God can make some improvements.

In my case, any of the following are red flags calling for lifestyle adjustment: an impatient, critical tongue and ready tears if I take on too much, expect too much, or for any reason feel overwhelmed; a tendency to obsess, i.e., to grind over the same thoughts repeatedly to no avail; and near-panic ("limited-symptom") attacks if fatigue, stress, and caffeine hit me all at once. **Taking time to rest and eat well (as Elijah did in his post-Mt. Carmel depression) and enjoy the Lord's company will usually correct the above. In addition I may say "no" to or cut back on some involvement. Basically I take a three-pronged approach: improve my own ability to function, check my standards for performance and the number of obligations I have to make sure I'm being realistic, and, make sure I'm not relying on myself too much and the Lord too little.**

As clinicians, we consider something to be a disorder when it causes significant distress or impairment of functioning in duties or relationships. A tendency is not the equivalent of a disorder; an occasional bad mood or fleeting episode of tension does not constitute sickness. Most people experience these or other annoyances or flaws. One element of good mental health is learning not to freak over these. God will forgive your sinful words, actions, and omissions, and help you break patterns (if you quit making excuses), or, for problems over which you have no control, He will give you sufficient grace to endure them, as He did with Paul for his thorn in the flesh (2 Cor. 12:9, 7).

Well and loving it.

Do I consider myself to have completely recovered? Yes, long ago. In 1986 or 1987, I realized that if I continued to see myself as a recovering mental patient, I would be doing myself a disservice; I was no longer recovering but growing. If you will recall the mental health continuum I described earlier, you will realize that even after you have crossed over that elusive line separating sickness from health, you still have plenty of room to grow towards complete health and wholeness. So I am still growing towards maturity and Christlikeness and will be until my death. I trust the promise that God will complete the work He has begun in us (Phil. 1:6).

God did deliver me from the depths of the pit in a way that I now see as miraculous. "Miraculous" is not synonymous with "instantaneous." A five-week turn-around after months or years of being messed up is a miracle in my opinion. My testimony is that God has brought me not only from sickness to health, but also from a life of weakness and fear into a life of confidence and courage; He gave me more than I asked for.

All things work together for good... (Rom. 8:28)

Since 1984 **I have had one brief episode of depression, and that was following a divorce in 1990**. John and I had had a rough year, and I was well aware of the strain, though I did not see the divorce coming. As soon as I knew John had filed, I set up an appointment with Dr. Mason. He put me on Elavil again, saying that since I already had a history of one depression, and a divorce can cause anybody to be depressed, it would be wise to take the precaution.

Mostly what I experienced that fall was a profound numbness and shock, and I cried easily. I took a break from graduate school for one semester until I could get some major decisions behind me and pull myself together. **The loss I had so desperately feared in 1984 was now upon me, and I survived without debilitating fear.** Heartbreak, yes; panic disorder, no. This time the Elavil caused me more trouble than it was worth, so I gradually weaned off of it and managed just fine.

I hope that the dissolution of my marriage with John does not alarm you about your own situation. **You can make a choice to handle things better than we did. Here is an over-simplified view of what transpired:** From 1984 to 1990, we did have many good times with each other, our sons, and our congregation. However, we still never completely put 1984 behind us. Even though John said I became vastly different in a positive way, his view of me as a person was never fully restored; and I did not accommodate his refusal to see and accept the real me. Knowing that he merely "allowed" me to live there as a second-class citizen really gnawed at me. My anger made its way into criticism and verbal outbursts towards him, which of course reinforced any negative views he did have of me and propelled a vicious cycle. Unfortunately, John's not knowing when I would next explode outweighed for him all the positive changes I had made.

189

I would have been open to discussion, but John had always found it difficult to hold conversations that might become uncomfortable, and any fears on his part that I might over-react would have made him even less likely to talk. He decided the situation was too difficult, and, instead of discussing it constructively, he ended it. While I agree that we desperately needed change, I have never felt that divorce was the only or ideal solution. The solution lay in mutual forgiveness and respect.

To the extent that I had been waiting for something I didn't get, I was still allowing circumstances to limit or determine my happiness. I could not reach my goal of un-qualified contentment unless I dropped such conditions.

Much has been made of forgiveness as a letting go of the need for revenge. I learned that forgiveness must also include a letting go of the expectation or need for the other person to make things right, e.g., by saying what we want to hear. Forgiveness is another no-matter-what proposition. Jesus did not say to forgive only after apologies or restitution. He simply said, "Forgive." Angry feelings may still arise occasionally, but do free yourself from the bondage of unmet "need"!

In case you feel discouraged by my marital outcome, **take heart from these things: my relationship with God and the lessons I had learned in the pit served me well during this time** (I also discovered Jeremiah 29:11-14, which reassured me that God was not finished with me yet); **God used this unfortunate event to bring about good**—more maturity in me, along with a realization that I needed to deal with some anger and **do some forgiving, which I finally did as I became more acutely aware of my *own* need for forgiveness; and my life was not over,** as God has continued to teach, mold, use, and bless me.

Another fresh start.

In 1991, I met and married Ray Tackett, who from the outset has had a refreshing perspective on and acceptance of my past and my personality. He sees mental illness as real and no more deserving of condemnation than physical illness. Besides, he is a humble person who would not be inclined to pass judgment on me for any reason. We also had the advantage of no difficult past to overcome—no hard feelings or painful memories. Ray and my sons were with me the day I received my M.S. in Clinical Psychology and have been supportive of my counseling career.

In recent years, I have continued to grow. **Having learned the high cost of resentment, I try with God's help not to carry grudges. Ray and I offer each other soft and tough love in an appropriately interdependent way. Many of the things I used to "try to do" I now just "do" naturally. And I am happy!** On top of my healing and my walk with the Lord, my cup is brimming over with other blessings: good relationships with Ray and my three sons, Joseph's conversion a few years after his brothers', an awesome step-son, three delightful daughters-in-law, a supportive extended family, and a satisfying career.

In addition to the areas I have already mentioned, I have found my life and health enhanced by learning more on these subjects: codependency and boundary-setting; tough love; personality types; the differences in communication styles and basic needs of men and women; spiritual warfare; spiritual gifts; suffering; and anger and forgiveness. Do not compulsively try to master each of these; allow God to direct YOU. Remember: God is the Healer, and growth is a process. May the testimony and lessons in this book lighten your steps and speed you on your journey!

It was good for me to be afflicted
so that I might learn your decrees.

Psalm 119:71

191

Chapter 23

Higher Ground

This chapter is simply a compilation of additional tips for recovery and growth. Start with this: If you haven't done so already, get a thorough physical exam. Then....

Fun and good for you, too:

Laugh heartily and often. Wholesome humor is therapeutic.

Plan pleasant activities to anticipate, then do them, so that when good feelings return, they have a reason to stay.

Savor the moment. Stop living only in yesterday or tomorrow.

Exercise regularly. Indoors is good; outdoors is better. Exercise stimulates the release of "feel-good" endorphins and improves circulation to the brain.

Act as if you already are the person you want to become.

Seek balance in many areas: work and play; self-awareness vs. lack of self-consciousness; expressing your feelings vs. absorbing them; thinking about living your life vs. living your life; focus on self vs. focus on others; saying "yes" and saying "no"; petitioning God vs. thanking Him for provisions He's already made and for answered prayer; focusing on Bible study vs. losing yourself in praising God; and doing your part while letting God do His.

In your relationships:

Remember that you are not God. You have limited control over your spouse and your children. God loves them even more than you do, so put them in His hands and leave them there.

When other people seem undeserving or unappreciative of all that you do, follow Colossians 3:23-24: "Whatever you do, work at it with all your heart, as working for the Lord, not for men, since you know that you will receive an inheritance from the Lord as a reward. It is the Lord Christ you are serving."

Stop overlooking your shortcomings while trying to change others; instead overlook others' faults and change yourself.

Remember that having the right to do something does not mean that to do it is right.

Learn the difference between being assertive and being aggressive, then be assertive in a discerning way.

When things go wrong.

Imagine what I call a "Catastrophe Scale," on which "10" represents a true catastrophe and "1" is no big deal When you feel yourself becoming upset or angry, stop and ask yourself where the present situation falls on this scale. In the big picture of your whole life, is it worth getting worked up over? You will find it wonderfully reinforcing to see how much self-control you actually do have. And the further good news is that even in a "10," you are not alone; God will strengthen you and even bring something good from the crisis, if you love Him.

As a friend of mine has said, "Keep one foot in heaven." If you keep your eyes on heavenly things, you will be less distressed when things go wrong here. Seen from heaven's vantage point, today's hardship is just a blip on a screen.

Avoid the three thoughts which Albert Ellis says are guaranteed to get you upset: the idea that things "must" go a certain way (usually the painless way or your chosen way); it will be "awful" if they do not go that way; and you will not be able to "stand it."

193

Things are not guaranteed to go your way on this earth; most happenings are not awful (though a few are); and your ability to endure hard knocks is greater than you think (Phil. 4:13).

If changing your thoughts does not keep you from getting angry, either express yourself in a constructive, assertive way, or internally release the anger, i.e., choose to let it go. And forgive.

Simplify.

If you tend to feel overwhelmed, focus on only the next fifteen minutes; use it well, and then tackle the next fifteen minutes. Many tasks do not take more time than this. You will build momentum, and the psychological effect is that you will feel you have accomplished something extra instead of running behind.

Unclutter your environment. Too much "stuff" around you can overwhelm the eye and constantly nag at you to dust and organize. My life feels less cluttered if my home is less cluttered.

Facing the tasks of the day.

If you are a compulsive doer, prioritize. Save the least important things for later, or lower the standards by which you plan to do them. When you begin to feel driven or dissatisfied, ask yourself, "If I don't get such-and-such done today, will it really matter ten years from now?" Use the catastrophe scale with that question. Most of what we fret over will have been forgotten by next week.

If you find yourself continually frustrated, lower your expectations in some areas, while increasing your confidence levels (in God and self), your performance, and your support system. That is, find a happy medium between what you expect to do and what you actually do. Don't over-simplify either by wiping out expectations altogether or by going to the other extreme and pushing yourself too hard.

Don't drive yourself with "should's," "ought to's," and "must's." You could drive yourself crazy with "A good mom should...." Even consistency, which is important in parenting, doesn't require perfection and rigidity. Be flexible sometimes. You and your family will benefit from a balance of predictability and variety.

Driven by compulsions?

"Need to" and "have to" are motivated by fear, or by the desperation to earn or prove something (this also usually has fear behind it). If you are consumed by such drives, ask God to reveal your motivation to you. Perhaps you are feverishly avoiding something that isn't catastrophic at all or that God could handle; or perhaps you are pursuing something that isn't important in the grand scheme of things.

Whatever you fear or run from has power over you. "A man is a slave to whatever has mastered him" (2 Pet. 2:19). Ideally, nothing has more control over us than the Holy Spirit does. Pray that your freedom in Christ would manifest itself in your areas of compulsion. And keep your mind on things of the Spirit, for this is "life and peace" (Rom. 8:6).

Find your peace in who Jesus is, who you are in him, and what your future is thanks to him. When Paul refers to a peace that transcends understanding (Phil. 4:7), he is saying that the world will not understand how you stay calm in the face of stress or disaster. Of course, you will not stay steady if you expect people or circumstances to be what makes you happy. If these can unsettle you greatly, then perhaps you are looking too much to them for happiness and contentment. People and life will let you down, while Jesus, who wants to give us "life to the full" (Jn. 10:10) and joy "made full" (Jn. 15:11), is "the same yesterday and today and forever" (Heb. 13:8). Look to him for joy and peace.

Once you have learned to find joy in Jesus, you may discover happiness in many other little things. Once you have learned the importance of truth, you will be amazed at the extent to which the Bible is a mental health manual. And once your heart is open, you will see God and learn of Him everywhere.

If you are fighting to make each moment count, i.e., if you have a hang-up about not wasting time, know that being and relating are as important as doing. Rest in God: remember that His acceptance of you depends on what Jesus has already accomplished, not what you may yet accomplish.

Still a little anxious?

If you are improving yet still have free-floating anxiety, pray, then do something else. It may dissipate in time as mine did.

Trust God for the grace to get through today. God wanted the wandering Israelites to learn that He would meet their needs as the needs arose and not before. Manna and meat would be provided daily. Don't try to live next week's trials with only today's grace. Also, God wanted the people to trust Him by remembering the provisions He had already made and the promises He had already kept. If you are looking for a new miracle, you may get one; *or* God may want you to look back at your life (or even your journal) and see the messages and answers to prayer He has already given you. These also build faith.

To be and feel stronger, do a Bible study on your identity in Christ and on spiritual warfare. Get a good concordance and look up such words as: overcome, victory, war, bold, conquer, courageous, victory, enemy, triumphant, fight, greater, and other forms of these words. You will be encouraged!

Grow in the grace and knowledge of our Lord and Savior Jesus Christ. To him be glory both now and forever! Amen.
(2 Pet. 3:18)

APPENDIX A

More on Depression, Anxiety, Panic, and Therapy

For the list of symptoms of various disorders which is consulted by mental health professionals, locate a *DSM-IV*, the *Diagnostic and Statistical Manual of Mental Disorders*, Fourth Edition. This book will also tell you the prevalence of each disorder, associated features, and its typical course.

Depression and anxiety.

You may not have all the symptoms which I had, especially if you are not suffering from both depression and anxiety, and you may not need all the tools mentioned in this book. [As an aside, I think I also met the criteria for Generalized Anxiety Disorder.] If you have Bipolar Disorder, you have additional symptoms beyond those for Major Depression. Bipolar has a more established genetic/chemical base, so medication may be essential. You will also benefit from straight thinking, healthier behavior, and a renewed spirit.

In a nutshell, recovery from depression or anxiety depends on the development of a healthy lifestyle: eat right, limit caffeine intake, get physical exercise and enough sleep, nurture good relationships, think realistically and rationally, handle your emotions effectively, actively love the Lord, and follow His instructions for living.

Tips on averting or coping with panic attacks (PAs).

1. Keep your general anxiety level low (see above).

2. When you sin or hurt someone, or someone has hurt you, clean the slate right away. Guilt and anger intensify PAs.

197

3. Let the facts about PAs sink in. PAs will NOT kill you. They do NOT represent a serious physical or mental problem. If you pass out, your breathing will automatically return to normal. PAs are caused by the fight-or-flight response kicking in at the wrong time, a normal process triggered unnecessarily. You would not be distressed over the same sensations during a true crisis or physical assault or vigorous physical activity, so don't catastrophize now. Perhaps your neurotransmitters and autonomic nervous system are jumpy and labile. The PA signifies nothing, no matter how terrifying and uncomfortable it feels. Think of it as a wave that washes over you rather than an attack that victimizes you.

4. Having accepted the above, when a PA occurs, do WHATEVER best allows you to short-circuit or endure it. For instance, talk to someone, use slow diaphragmatic breathing, take a walk, mop the floor, hug someone, pray, tell Satan to get lost, or consciously relax your muscles (Progressive Muscle Relaxation trains you in this). Use positive self-talk, e.g., "This will pass," There's nothing seriously wrong with me," "Panic attacks never killed anyone," or "I can endure this—I have before." Or imagine a peaceful place or meditate on scripture—do anything except think about how awful you feel or how deadly this seems.

5. Stop worrying about when the next PA will occur. Tell yourself PAs are one of many nuisances that afflict human beings and you will manage with God's help if one does occur. Plan your life as if you had no PAs. Consider this: would you prefer *a narrow, boring existence* with occasional PAs, or *a life of interesting experiences* with occasional PAs?

If you have been avoiding certain places and activities because you've panicked there before, start going and doing again, beginning with the least alarming scenario first, for a brief period or taking someone with you for a while; then gradually tackle more. As you do this repeatedly, the evidence should help you come and go more naturally and feel less anxious, because you will see: "I don't panic every time after all," or "I didn't go crazy," or "Even though I panicked, the rest of the experience was worth it." Even if you do panic and make a quick exit or do something embarrassing, on the catastrophe scale how awful is that really? You will begin to feel more competent and normal as you maintain a more normal lifestyle.

Cognitive-behavior therapy (CBT).

Cognitive therapy focuses on the examination of one's beliefs, assumptions, expectations, attributions, and automatic thoughts, and testing the evidence to see which of these is supported and which should be changed. Behavior therapy focuses on directly changing behavior by manipulating the cues or triggers and/or the consequences of behavior, or by changing the behavior in the imagination first or in real but graduated steps. BT may include modeling, education, and training in problem-solving and decision-making. Both therapies usually involve homework. CBT combines the two approaches.

Is CBT Biblical? Certainly. Jesus didn't talk much about feelings. His teachings were directed toward changing the way people thought, acted, and related to each other. Of course, his starting place for this was that they would surrender their prideful, selfish attitudes and let him be the Lord of their lives. Our only hope of consistent and permanent change in how we think, speak, act, and relate is by changing who we are, and we do that by becoming new persons in Christ.

APPENDIX B

If You Are Not a Christian

If you are not a Christian and would like to be (or are unsure), your interest suggests that God is beckoning you, because Jesus said that no one draws near to him unless God first draws the person (Jn. 6:44).

If you are seeking to become a Christian or to be sure that you already are, here is where you begin: You would first need to accept that Jesus is the Son of God (meaning he has the same divine nature as his Father) who died in your place. Why in your place? Our sin separates us from a loving but just God who cannot allow sin into His presence. None of us could ever be good enough to close the gap between us and God (Rom. 3:23), so God sent Jesus to do that. Because Jesus was perfect, the sacrifice of his life could accomplish something special, which was to close the gap, to make possible a relationship with God here on earth and later in heaven for anyone who humbly accepts this "redemption" or "ransom" on their own behalf.

So, in addition to acknowledging who Jesus is, to become a Christian you would confess your sinfulness to God, repent, and thank Him for making your redemption possible. To repent means to be so sorry for your sins that you want to live differently from now on. When we realize that our sin is such a serious matter to God that it took a death to undo the consequences, it is not hard to see sin as something that should be abandoned. If you have done the above, sincerely and humbly, you have accepted Jesus as your Savior.

Don't stop there, though. To attempt to abandon sin and pride without having something to replace them would be an exercise in futility, so God provided a superior alternative in

Jesus's life and teachings. Furthermore, because Jesus is alive and well (thanks to the resurrection), you can have a relationship with him so that you're not going it alone.

So it works like this: you personally invite Jesus (in prayer) to be the Lord of your life, meaning you commit to living his way instead of your own, and you invite his spirit (the Holy Spirit) to come into your mind and heart to help you do this. It makes sense to put your life in the hands of someone who loves you more than you love yourself, knows you better than you know yourself, and can see your future more clearly than you can. The Holy Spirit will give you the strength, love, and wisdom you need to follow Jesus's teachings and be more like him. If you're afraid that you will still fall short, have confidence in 1 John 1:9, which says that if you sin and will confess it, God "is faithful and just to forgive us our sin and purify us of all unrighteousnesss."

If you have accepted Jesus as your Savior and invited him to be your Lord, you should tell at least one other living soul. Romans 10:9 says, "If you confess with your mouth 'Jesus is Lord,' and believe in your heart that God raised him from the dead, you will be saved."

Also, anyone who is serious about being a Christian should learn more about God's Word and be baptized (this symbolizes your inner cleansing). Find a group of believers who take the Bible seriously and who will love you and make real for you the saying that "Joys shared are joys multiplied, and sorrows shared are sorrows divided." By the way, if you have had trouble understanding Bible passages in the past, you will find that with the Holy Spirit in your life, things start to make a lot more sense.

If you have just become a Christian and you don't feel any different, trust that you *are* different. Remember all I said earlier about feelings not being a good yardstick for reality. If you have accepted Jesus as your Savior and Lord, you have "passed out of death into life" (Jn. 5:24). If you believe "in the name of the Son of God...you may know that you have eternal life" (1 Jn. 5:13). If any one is "in Christ, he is a new creation; the old has gone, the new has come" (2 Cor. 5:17). Your confidence that you are "saved" is based on God's promises, which make no mention of your emotions. As the song says, we know that Jesus loves us because "the Bible tells me so," not because "my feelings tell me so."

Can a non-Christian recover from mental illness? She can recover enough to cross that elusive line between sickness and health, but she will not reach her full potential. She can take medication, grasp some truth, and make some changes in behavior by her own efforts. However, if she could also be sure of more lasting change, have joy and life that are eternal, and be loved by Someone unconditionally while she is still a work in progress, why would she settle for anything less?

Any one seeking mental health is seeking life in all its abundance; that person needs a path to walk *in* and solid ground to walk *on*. Jesus is "the way, the truth, and the life" (Jn. 14:6), the destination, the route, and the provisions for the journey all rolled into one.

However, avoid tapping into God as a resource to help you reach your own selfishly-devised goals. God does want to heal and help you, but in exchange for listening and responding to you, He also hopes you will listen and respond to Him. Real relationships are two-way.

And that is the bottom line. **Being a Christian is not so much a matter of *knowing about Jesus* as it is *knowing Jesus*.** The Christian life is a life of loving relationships with God and with people. What is more important than that?

APPENDIX C

Recommended Reading

You may find that, in addition to the resources included in the Reference List, the following are also helpful:

Alberti, Robert E., and Michael L. Emmons. 1990. *Your Perfect Right*. San Luis Obispo, CA: Impact Publishers.

Anderson, Neil. 1993. *The Bondage Breaker*. Eugene, OR: Harrison House Publishers.

_____. 1990. *Victory Over the Darkness*. Ventura, CA: Regal Books.

Beattie, Melody. 1992. *Codependent No More*. Center City, MN: Hazelden.

Billheimer, Paul E. 1977. *Don't Waste Your Sorrows*. Minneapolis: Bethany House Publishers; Fort Washington, PA: Christian Literature Crusade.

Cannon, Carol. 1993. *Never Good Enough*. Boise, ID: Pacific Press Publishing Association.

Carter, Les. 1983. *Good 'n' Angry*. Grand Rapids, MI: Baker Book House.

_____, and Frank Minirth. 1995. *The Freedom From Depression Workbook*. Nashville: Thomas Nelson Publishers.

Cloud, Henry, and John Townsend. 1992. *Boundaries*. Grand Rapids, MI: Zondervan Publishing House.

Littauer, Florence. 1986. *Blow Away the Black Clouds*. Eugene,

OR: Harvest House Publishers.

_____. 1992. *Personality Plus*. Grand Rapids, MI: Fleming H. Revell.

Mantell, Michael R. 1988. *Don't Sweat the Small Stuff*. San Luis Obispo, CA: Impact Publishers.

McCullough, Michael E., Steven J. Sandage, and Everett L. Worthington. 1997. *To Forgive Is Human*. Downers Grove, IL: InterVarsity Press.

McGee, Robert S., and Pat Springle. 1992. *Getting Unstuck*. Dallas: Word Publishing.

Meyer, Joyce. 1995. *Battlefield of the Mind*. Tulsa, OK: Harrison House.

Minirth, Frank, Paul Meier, and Don Hawkins. 1989. *Worry-free Living*. Nashville: Thomas Nelson, Inc.

Oliver, Gary J., and H. Norman Wright. 1995. *Good Women Get Angry*. Ann Arbor, MI: Vine Books.

Seamands, David A. 1985. *Healing of Memories*. Wheaton, IL: Victor Books.

Sledge, Tim. 1992. *Making Peace with Your Past*. Nashville: LifeWay Press.

Smedes, Lewis B. 1984. *Forgive & Forget: Healing the Hurts We Don't Deserve*. New York: Pocket Books.

GROW groups exist in three states. To locate a group, call:
(Ill.) Champaign 217-352-6989'   (R. I.) 401-464-3137
(N. J.) Glassboro 856-881-2008 or Neptune City 732-775-5604

Reference List

Allender, Dan B. 1992. *The Wounded Heart*. Colorado Springs: NavPress.

American Psychiatric Association. 1994. *Diagnostic and Statistical Manual of Mental Disorders*, Fourth Edition. Washington, D.C.: American Psychiatric Association.

Antonuccio, David O., William G. Danton, and Garland Y. DeNelsky. 1995. Psychotherapy versus medication for depression: Challenging the conventional wisdom with data. *Professional Psychology: Research and Practice* 26:574-585.

_____, Michael Thomas, and William G. Danton. 1997. A cost-effectiveness analysis of cognitive behavior therapy and fluoxetine (Prozac) in the treatment of depression. *Behavior Therapy* 28:187-210.

Barchas, Jack D., Peter M. Marzuk, and Ronna Henry Siegel. 1998. General psychiatry. *JAMA* vol. 280 n. 11:961-962.

Beattie, Melody. 1994. *The Lessons of Love*. SanFrancisco: Harper.

Beck, A.T., A.J. Rush, B.F. Shaw, and G. Emery. 1979. *Cognitive Therapy of Depression*. New York: Guilford Press.

Beck, Judith S. 1995. *Cognitive Therapy: Basics and Beyond*. New York: Guilford Press.

Begley, Sharon. 1998. Is everybody crazy? *Newsweek*. 26 Jan.

Bourne, Edmund J. 1990. *The Anxiety & Phobia Workbook*. Oakland, CA: New Harbinger Publications, Inc.

Burns, David D. 1980. *Feeling Good: The New Mood Therapy*. New York: NAL Penguin, Inc.

Buscaglia, Leo F. 1982. *Living, Loving, & Learning*. New York: Fawcett Columbine.

Charlotte's Web. 1973. Paramount Pictures. A motion picture.

Cloud, Henry, and John Townsend. 1994. *False Assumptions*. Grand Rapids, MI: Zondervan Publishing House.

Cry Freedom. 1987. Marble Arch/Universal Studios. A motion picture.

Davis, Martha, Elizabeth Robbins Eshelman, and Matthew McKay. 1988. *The Relaxation & Stress Reduction Workbook*. Oakland, CA: New Harbinger Publications.

Dobson, James. 1993. *When God Doesn't Make Sense*. Wheaton, IL: Tyndale House Publishers, Inc.

Ellis, Albert, and Robert A. Harper. 1975. *A New Guide to Rational Living*. Englewood Cliffs, NJ: Prentice-Hall.

Epictetus. 1899. *The Works of Epictetus*. Boston: Little, Brown.

Forrest Gump. 1994. Paramount Pictures. A motion picture.

GROW, Inc. 1982. *GROW: The Program of Growth to Maturity*. Sydney, Australia: GROW Publications.

Groundhog Day. 1993. Columbia Pictures. A motion picture.

Gulley, Philip. 1997. *Front Porch Tales*. Sisters, OR: Multnomah Books.

Indiana Jones and the Last Crusade. 1989. LucasFilms. A motion picture.

Johnson, Barbara. 1990. *Stick a Geranium in Your Hat and Be Happy*. Dallas: Word Publishing.

_____. 1992. *Splashes of Joy in the Cesspools of Life*. Dallas: Word Publishing.

LaHaye, Tim. 1974. *How to Win Over Depression*. Grand Rapids, Mich.: Zondervan Publishing House.

Lucado, Max. 1994. *When God Whispers Your Name*. Dallas: Word Publishing.

Mary Poppins. 1964. Walt Disney. A motion picture.

Maxwell, John. 1994. *Five Things I Know About People*. Colorado Springs: Focus on the Family. Audiocassette.

McGee, Robert S. 1992. *Search for Significance*, LIFE Support Edition. Nashville: LifeWay Press.

Minirth, Frank B. and Paul D. Meier. 1988. *Happiness Is A Choice*. Grand Rapids, MI: Baker Book House.

Nine to Five. 1980. IPC Films. A motion picture.

Old Yeller. 1957. Walt Disney. A motion picture.

Peck, M. Scott. 1978. *The Road Less Traveled*. New York: Simon & Schuster.

Pollyanna. 1960. Walt Disney. A motion picture.

The Right Stuff. 1983. Ladd Company. A motion picture.

Robin Hood. 1973. Walt Disney. A motion picture.

The Santa Clause. 1994. Walt Disney. A motion picture.

Seamands, David A. 1991. *Healing for Damaged Emotions*.
 Wheaton, IL: Victor Books.

Simon, Sidney B., Leland W. Howe, and Howard Kirschenbaum.
 1972. *Values Clarification: A Handbook of Practical
 Strategies for Teachers and Students*. New York: Hart
 Publishing.

Smalley, Gary, and John Trent. 1991. *Love Is a Decision*.
 Phoenix AZ: Today's Family. Live seminar video series.

The Sound of Music. 1965. 20th Century Fox. A motion picture.

Ten Boom, Corrie, and John Sherrill. 1974. *The Hiding Place*.
 New York: Bantam Books.

Thurman, Chris. 1989. *The Lies We Believe*. Nashville: Thomas
 Nelson Publisher.

_____. 1991. *The Truths We Must Believe*. Nashville:
 Thomas Nelson Publisher.

Yancey, Philip. 1988. *Disappointment With God: Three
 Questions No One Asks Aloud*. Grand Rapids, MI: Zondervan
 Publishing House.

Further source information unknown:
 Rockome Gardens sign
 Serenity Prayer by Reinhold Niebuhr
 "Attitude" by Chuck Swindoll
 "Let Go and Let God" poem